JOHN KINROSS

Discovering
Castles in England and Wales

SHIRE PUBLICATIONS LTD

The cover illustration is of Orford Castle, Suffolk.

British Library Cataloguing in Publication Data
Kinross, John, 1933—
   Discovering castles in England and Wales.
   — 2nd ed. — (Discovering; v.152)
   1. Castles — England — Guide-books
   I. Title II. Series
   914.2'04858 DA660
   ISBN 0-85263-686-5

Set in 9 point Times roman and printed in Great Britain by C. I. Thomas
& Sons (Haverfordwest) Ltd, Press Buildings, Merlins Bridge, Haverfordwest, Dyfed SA61 1XE.

Contents

CONTENTS

Castles of Wales

Acknowledgements

Photographs are acknowledged as follows: Hallam Ashley, plate 19; Alfred E. Bristow, plate 36; British Tourist Authority, plate 31; English Heritage, plate 11; George H. Haines, plate 39; John Kinross, plates 23, 44, 45, 54; M. D. Kinross, plate 32; Cadbury Lamb, plates 1, 5-7, 12-16, 18, 24-6, 29, 30, 34, 35, 37, 38, 41-3, 46-9, 51, 52, 55, 56 and front cover; John MacCormack, plates 2-4; Northumberland County Council, plates 20-2; John Vince, plate 9; Welsh Office, plate 50; Jeffery W. Whitelaw, plate 8; Geoffrey N. Wright, plate 17; *Yorkshire Post* and *Yorkshire Evening Post*, plates 27, 33. The ground plans of the four castles on pages 6 and 7 are Crown Copyright and reproduced by permission of English Heritage (Middleham, Berkhamsted) and the Welsh Office (Conwy, Harlech).

The author and publishers acknowledge with gratitude the assistance and co-operation of B. J. Stanier, formerly of the Ministry of Public Building and Works, and D. L. Pattison BA in editing this book. Thanks are also due to the many owners, administrators and custodians of castles who kindly assisted in the preparation of the text, and especially to the following: T. H. McK. Clough, Keeper, Rutland County Museum; John Evans, Pembokeshire Coast National Park Department; Wilfred Fattorini, Thomas Fattorini Ltd, Skipton Castle; Dr Stephen Hall, Boarstall Tower; Dr B. E. Harris, Editor, *Victoria History of Cheshire;* John Houghton, General Administrator, Sussex Archaeological Society; Derek W. Humphreys, Custodian, Tretower Castle; R. Jones, Sales Manager, Carisbrooke Castle Museum; R. A. Kennedy, Curator, Pembrokeshire Museums, Haverfordwest; R. W. Puttock, Comptroller, Arundel Castle; The Lord Saye and Sele, Broughton Castle; Miss M. Stinson, Pontefract Castle; Tim Tatton-Brown, Director, Canterbury Archaeological Trust; Commander Michael Saunders Watson DL, Rockingham Castle.

Introduction

The Romans brought military order to Britain with their legions, their great wall and their roads. They built the first stone forts, often on a river crossing or place of similar importance. The Saxon Shore forts were castles of a kind. Richborough and Burgh stand today with their massive walls and Dover has always been a military stronghold; their camps were made with earth or wooden walls, as at Launceston (Cornwall).

The Normans were the first people to build what we call castles, that is a fortified house or fortress used for defence purposes and built for a nobleman or a king. The earliest motte and bailey castles were simple wooden structures on top of a mound or motte together with some form of palisade, with a ditch round the motte, not always filled with water, and sometimes round the bailey as well. They must have been uncomfortable places to inhabit and the ring forts like Old Sarum offered considerably more protection from bad weather.

Pevensey was built on the site of a Roman fort and the Normans merely used the fort as an outer bailey for animals, adding a square keep. In the thirteenth century the extra inner bailey curtain with its half-moon bastions and moat was added so that the castle became twice as strong. The fact that it was fortified in 1940 with machine-gun posts proves that the builders did their work well. At Portchester the same thing occurs but a square keep was constructed and the moat is not so impressive.

Rectangular keeps had insufficient living space and this may have prompted castle builders to design shell-keeps. Windsor and Restormel are good examples. The dwellings were arranged on the inside of the wall with a guard walk round the top of the curtain. Conisbrough keep has a chapel built into its walls and is immensely strong. The bailey towers here are solid and it was a natural step to make them hollow as with the Pevensey inner bailey or at White Castle (Gwent).

The Edwardian castles are utterly different from any others. The unruly Welsh were conquered in 1282 but Edward I wanted to prevent further outbreaks of trouble. The few loyal settlements needed protection and Conwy and Caernarfon are perfect examples of fortified towns, with the castle walls playing a vital part in the defensive system. Harlech was an exception because it is built on a rock and is accessible from one side only and that is protected by the gatehouse.

With the increase of military inventiveness, cannon became more powerful and the mighty walls of Norham crumbled under Mons Meg's cannonballs. The answer was to build bastions and widen the moats. Henry VIII's forts are the obvious step. The

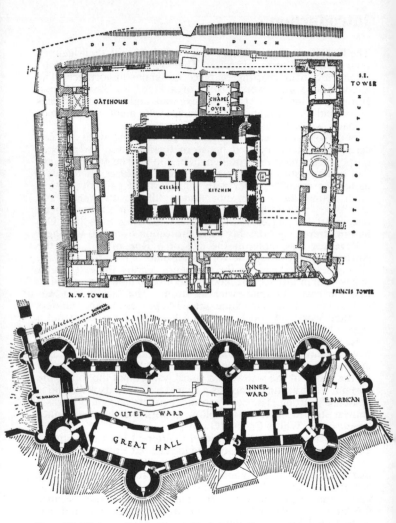

Top: Middleham Castle, North Yorkshire. The twelfth-century keep is one of the largest in England and incorporates the great hall. Bottom: Conwy Castle, Gwynedd, stands at the mouth of the river; its walls played a vital part in the defence of the town, which was loyal to Edward I at the time of the Welsh uprising.

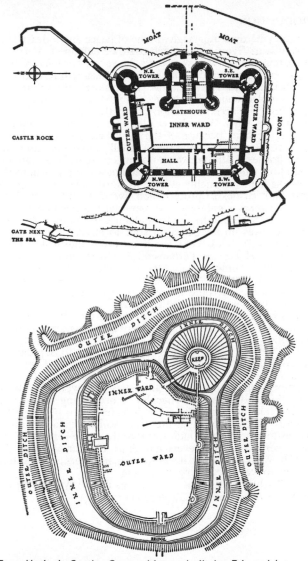

Top: Harlech Castle, Gwynedd was built by Edward I on a rock overlooking the sea with its gatehouse on the town side. Bottom: Berkhamsted Castle, Hertfordshire. Little remains of this castle today but the rare double moat is of great interest.

inner bailey became a passage in time of peace and a death trap in time of war. Every square inch could be defended. Very few large castles of this type were built, however, because by then the castle had gone out of fashion. Queen Elizabeth I's Star Fort in the Scillies and Hurst Castle (Hampshire) are impressive gunnery emplacements. Pendennis and St Mawes (Cornwall) are equally fine but accommodation is strictly limited.

During the Civil War the castles that put up the longest resistance, perhaps because of the stout hearts of their defenders, were Pembroke and a few small, relatively unknown fortified houses: Lathom, which no longer exists, Boarstall and Donnington, which consist of tall gatehouses today, where the earthworks kept the enemy at bay. In Northumberland humble farmers built castles to protect their livestock and themselves. The peel tower was enlarged and haphazard castles like Sizergh appeared. In Scotland the French influence was more prevalent. Hermitage owes no allegiance in style to anything built a few miles away in England. Yet it is a home inside four walls, which is the essence of a castle. Perhaps this is why the most appealing ruins are the homely ones, the semi-fortified homes like Stokesay and Markenfield. These are the essence of English architecture, the outcome of years of defensive thought, the dream of every would-be castle owner.

Castles which are under the care of the Historic Buildings and Monuments Commission (English Heritage) are normally open at the following standard hours: March, April and October, weekdays 9.30 to 5.30, Sundays 2 to 5.30; May to September, weekdays 9.30 to 7, Sundays 2 to 7; November to February, weekdays 9.30 to 4, Sundays 2 to 4; closed 24th to 26th December. Times of opening of all castles, however, are subject to alteration and should be checked before setting out to visit them. The telephone number of English Heritage is 01-734 6010. The phrase 'open throughout the year', which appears in many of the castle descriptions, indicates that the castle is open to the public at certain times in every month of the year although the days of the week, as well as the hours, when visitors are admitted are likely to vary according to season.

Many Castles in Wales are cared for by Cadw: Welsh Historic Monuments (telephone: 0222 465511).

Castles of England

BEDFORDSHIRE

Someries

Leaving Luton by B653, the road to the Vauxhall car factory, the entrance gates to Luton Hoo are straight ahead at a double bend. Less than a mile on is a small road to the left that goes under the railway. At the top of the hill is a farm and a rough track to the left. The brick-built castle gatehouse is in farmland at the end of the track. The remains of the moat are in the field to the north-west.

Someries was founded by Sir John Rotherham, steward to the household of Henry III, on a site once used by Falk de Brent, who was the owner of Bedford Castle and one of King John's most loyal supporters. In 1406 Henry IV granted Luton manor to the Duke of Bedford and later it was acquired by Sir John Wenlock. Sir John was a friend of the great Earl of Warwick during the Wars of the Roses and at one time owned Berkhamsted Castle. Wenlock was a notorious turncoat; he fought for the Lancastrians in 1455 at St Albans, where he was seriously wounded; then espousing the Yorkist cause, he distinguished himself fighting for them at Towton but finally rejoined Warwick and led one third of the Lancastrian army at Tewkesbury in 1471. Here he was killed, supposedly by his own side.

According to Leland, Wenlock's heir, who married a relation of the Archbishop of York, inherited 'three hundred makes of land...and a fair place within the parish of Luton called Somerys, which was sumptuously begun by Lord Wenlock (in 1448) but not finished.' Until about 1700 Somerys or Someries was an important building, more of a fortified manor than a house, but the Napier family who acquired it preferred Luton Hoo and they dismantled the high tower.
Unrestricted access.

BERKSHIRE

Donnington

Just outside Newbury, off the Oxford road, the two drum towers of Donnington Castle's gatehouse stand on the top of the castle mound, having survived a furious bombardment during the Civil War. Donnington was owned by John Packer, a Parliamentarian, but, as it was near to Oxford, Charles I seized it and put in a garrison of two hundred men and four cannon under Sir John Boys. A four star breastwork was constructed round the castle, with a gap for the road, which in those days ran past the gatehouse. In 1644 Boys resisted two attempts to take the castle and it was the centre of the second battle of Newbury. Waller attempted to make the castle surrender by poisoning the well but Boys sent forty musketeers to clean it and dig it deeper. In 1646 Colonel Dalbier was given the task of reducing the castle, and with a massive mortar he proceeded to batter down the walls. In spite of a royalist sortie by Captain Donne that killed eighty men and captured sixty, Boys knew he must soon surrender. A message from the king at Oxford suggested he obtain the best conditions he could and on 1st April the castle surrendered, each man taking his arms and ammunition and marching to Walling-ford.

The Packers continued to live here until the construction of the new house next door. Later the property passed to the Hartleys and in 1946 it was taken over by the Ministry of Works. *English Heritage. Open throughout the year.*

Windsor

England's largest castle was originally constructed by William the Conqueror on a chalk cliff overlooking the Thames. The site was 3 miles (5 km) from the original Saxon settlement at Old Windsor where Edward the Confessor had his hunting lodge. The stone castle was erected by Henry II on the site of William's large motte. There are three baileys — lower, middle and upper — and the total area is 13 acres (5.3 ha).

Prince John garrisoned it during Richard I's absence but was forced to yield it to Queen Eleanor. Henry III built the west wall and its towers flanking the main street. The first chapel was built where the Albert Memorial Chapel stands. This was made the centre of the new Order of the Garter by Edward III, who established a college with poor knights to organise the Order. The Norman gate and more domestic buildings were built at this time. St George's Chapel was started in 1475 by Edward IV and completed by Henry VII. The body of Henry VI was moved from Chertsey to the chapel in 1485.

Elizabeth I added the gallery, which now forms part of the library, and the North Terrace, which was built so that the queen could reach the Home Park without going through the State Apartments. The latter were rebuilt by Hugh May for Charles II and craftsmen such as Verrio and Grinling Gibbons worked on the interior decoration. The famous Long Walk was laid out at this time. The next king to alter the castle was George III, who lowered one of the walls and erected a new window in the chapel, of which Walpole said, 'The Lord appears to be trying to get to heaven in a hurry'. George IV brought in Sir Jeffrey

Wyatville, who doubled the height of the Round Tower, changed the skyline with new towers, made a new sunken garden and altered the State Apartments. Queen Victoria turned the old chapel into a memorial chapel for Prince Albert and a small chapel has been built to the memory of George VI.

Castle precincts open daily. State Apartments, Queen Mary's Dolls' House, Royal Mews Exhibition, Curfew Tower, Albert Memorial Chapel and St George's Chapel open throughout the year, except certain holidays, but the Curfew Tower is closed on Sundays and Mondays, the Albert Memorial Chapel on Sundays, and the State Apartments when the Queen is in residence.

BUCKINGHAMSHIRE

Boarstall

Boarstall Tower consists of an early fourteenth-century gatehouse guarding the bridge over the moat. Windows were inserted probably in the sixteenth and seventeenth centuries and one side of the moat was filled in and replaced by a wall about 1670. During the Civil War there were three distinct sieges, the place being finally taken by the Parliamentary forces after the capture of the king.

National Trust. Wednesday afternoons, during the summer, by written permission only.

CAMBRIDGESHIRE

Cambridge

Built in 1068 on the north bank of the river, Cambridge Castle was destroyed by Cromwell during the Civil War.

The motte stands in front of the County Council offices.

Kimbolton

This was the ancient seat of the Mandevilles and Montagus. The present 'castle' was refaced and largely remodelled by Vanbrugh and the fourth Earl and fifth Duke of Manchester between 1707 and 1720. It is now a school.

Open occasionally during spring and summer.

Longthorpe

Near Peterborough, Longthorpe Tower was added to the manor in 1300. It has unusual fourteenth-century wall paintings of biblical scenes.

English Heritage. Open throughout the year.

CHESHIRE

Beeston

Situated on the A49, Beeston is about half way between Crewe and Chester. The castle stands on top of a 500 foot (150 m) sandstone crag, approachable only from the south. In 1220 Ranulf de Blundeville, sixth Earl of Chester, built his castle here where he could command the country around and levy his land tax. In 1264 Beeston was occupied by Simon de Montfort for a year, and in 1399 Richard II, on his way to Flint, left his treasure here, where it was soon collected by Henry Bolingbroke as Henry IV.

During the Civil War Beeston was occupied by the Roundheads. It was attacked by a small party of Royalists, under Captain Landford, who climbed the north wall and got into the upper ward. Captain Steel, the governor, surrendered and shortly after was shot by his own men in Nantwich. The Royalists were besieged in 1644 but held out until November 1645, when they marched out under their commander, Captain Valet. The slighting that took place in 1646 was very thorough. *English Heritage. Open throughout the year.*

Chester

This was once an important walled town with a castle, but although the city walls remain, only the twelfth-century 'Agricola's Tower' has survived from the medieval castle. Chester was a Roman fortress, strengthened by the Saxons and by the Normans, who built a motte and bailey castle. From the time of Edward of Caernarfon (1301) the eldest son of the sovereign has usually been created Earl of Chester. In the late eighteenth and early nineteenth centuries, the present gateway, military quarters and assize courts were built. The Cheshire Military Museum in 'A' Block displays the Colours and Standards and other regimentalia of the 22nd (Cheshire) Regiment, 5th Royal Inniskilling Dragoon Guards, 3rd Carabiniers and the Cheshire (Earl of Chester's) Yeomanry.
Museum open throughout the year.

CORNWALL

Ince

Near Antony House (National Trust), Ince was a seventeenth-century castle, fortified during the Civil War for the king and later turned into a farmhouse. It was restored in 1920 and is a private house.
Viscount Boyd of Merton. Grounds open in summer under the National Gardens Scheme.

Launceston

Robert de Mortain built the first castle on the high hill above the town. It was probably of wood and was not replaced by stone until Richard of Cornwall obtained the property and built the shell-keep with a round tower inside and a strongly protected passage to the curtain from the gatehouse. This design is unusual in English castles. The space between the central tower and the curtain could be roofed over to permit extra fighting space if there was a siege. The central tower has a fireplace. Later an extra building was added as a jail.

The east gate contains the constable's quarters and here, under the gatehouse, is a room where George Fox, the Quaker, was imprisoned in 1656 for wearing his hat in court. During the Civil War, although ruined, the castle changed hands five times. The outer ward was still enclosed at the time but has long since been encroached upon by the town.

English Heritage. Open throughout the year.

Pendennis

Pendennis and St Mawes castles were built by Henry VIII in 1548 to protect Carrick Roads at Falmouth. Pendennis stands 300 feet (90 m) above the sea and consists of a circular tower 56 feet (17 m) in diameter, with walls 11 feet (3.35 m) thick pierced in three tiers with embrasures for guns. In Elizabeth I's reign a large angular rampart wall was added, covering nearly 2 acres (0.8 ha). The entrance is across a drawbridge from Castle Drive and through a gateway over which the arms of Henry VIII are prominently displayed.

During the Civil War Colonel Arundel of Trerice was the governor. He had anticipated a siege and had strengthened the defences with a pentagonal redoubt and other earthworks, constructed so that enemy cannon could not approach within range. Provisions for nine months were stored inside and the garrison consisted of eight hundred men. When Fairfax arrived in March 1646 Arundel refused to surrender and held out until 17th August, by which time his supplies had run out and two hundred of his men had fallen sick. Only Raglan in Gwent held out longer, but only two days longer.

There is a fine collection of arms and armour inside the castle and in the Elizabethan part there is a youth hostel.

English Heritage. Open throughout the year.

Restormel

The most picturesque castle in England, Restormel was built by Baldwin Fitzturstin, owner of Bordardle manor. In 1100 it passed to the Lord of Cardinham, whose grandson Robert was a king's justice. In 1270 it became the property of Richard, Earl of Cornwall, and since 1299 has belonged to the Duchy of Cornwall. Originally an earthwork, the gate was built up in 1100 and Robert was responsible for the circular curtain wall. This forms a keep on its own and the buildings erected inside were of a later date, the chapel projecting on the east and an arch being cut through the curtain for access. The east window was blocked during the Civil War when the chapel became a gun emplacement and look-out post.

English Heritage. Open throughout the year.

St Mawes

Begun in 1540 and considered the finest of Henry VIII's coastal forts, St Mawes lies across the estuary from Pendennis and Falmouth. It took three years to build and consists of a large central tower, surmounted by a small watch-tower, and three semicircular bastions arranged in a clover-leaf shape. A drawbridge, protected by musket loops and an outer blockhouse, leads to the first floor.

The Vyvyan family held the office of governor until 1632. The post was abolished in 1849. The castle now stands in gardens, but during the Second World War it was an important part of the coastal defences of Falmouth.

English Heritage. Open throughout the year.

St Michael's Mount

Opposite Marazion, the island of St Michael's Mount rises high out of the water some 600 yards (550 m) from the mainland. It is said to be part of the lost kingdom of Lyonesse and as early as 1044 was associated with Mont St Michel in France when a Benedictine monastery was formed here, a cell of the French monastery.

The first person to realise the military importance of the island was Henry de Pomeroy from Berry Pomeroy (Devon), who landed here in Richard I's reign with a force disguised as monks. They seized the island in the name of Prince John and remained there until Richard's return, when the Archbishop of Canterbury successfully led his troops against them.

The same ruse was used in the fifteenth century when John de Vere, Earl of Oxford, after escaping from the battlefield of Barnet in 1471, made his way to Wales and sailed round the coast to capture the Mount. He fortified it and eventually surrendered on honourable terms to Edward IV.

During the Civil War the Mount was garrisoned by the

Royalists under Sir Francis Basset, who spent most of his own money on the provisions. The Mount was used as a jail for important prisoners, including the Duke of Hamilton and the Royalist Sir Richard Grenville, who was arrested by his own side for insubordination to Sir Ralph Hopton. When Parliamentary troops moved in they found fifteen guns and four hundred stands of arms. From the Restoration the Mount belonged to the St Aubyn family. The Lady Chapel has been converted into Gothic-style drawing rooms. The refectory is known as the Chevy Chase Room because of its plaster frieze executed during the Civil War. A north wing was erected in 1927. There are no visible remains of the twelfth-century building.

National Trust. Open April to October, Mondays, Tuesdays, Wednesdays and Fridays (free flow); November to March, conducted tours on Monday, Wednesday and Friday, weather and tide permitting (no ferry service).

Tintagel

The site of King Arthur's legendary castle on the edge of the cliff, the ruins today are of the great hall, probably built in 1145 by Reginald, Earl of Cornwall. Henry III's brother Richard added an outer ward connected by a drawbridge to the island ward. It also had a fortified landing-stage.

English Heritage. Open throughout the year.

Trematon

An interesting shell-keep castle similar to Restormel, Trematon used to belong to the Duchy of Cornwall but is now in private hands. *Not open to the public.*

ISLES OF SCILLY

Cromwell's Castle

Built in 1651, Cromwell's Castle is a round tower and forebuilding on the west coast of Tresco. It is remarkably well preserved and is worth visiting. It had a garrison of twenty men and was supplied from St Mary's by sea. The entrance was by a wooden ladder.

King Charles's Castle

Built before Cromwell's Castle on the main Tresco cliff, it was converted into a fort during the Civil War and possibly the stones were taken away to build Cromwell's Castle.

Star Castle

On the island of St Mary's, Star Castle was built by Robert Adams, a surveyor, in 1593. It is an eight-pointed building surrounded by a rampart wall. It had gun embrasures and inside were a basement and two storeys. It had a garrison of twenty-five in 1637 with a further twenty-five Cornishmen for six months. Charles I came here, when prince, with the Duke of Buckingham. It has a gateway defended by a portcullis and an eighteenth-century bell tower. After its capture by Parliament in 1646 Star Castle was used as a prison for the Duke of Hamilton and other Royalists. In 1660 Sir Harry Vane was imprisoned here by Charles II, who knew the building well. In 1669 there was a garrison of two hundred men and later it was used as the governor's residence. Today Star Castle is a hotel.

CUMBRIA

Appleby

Founded, like Brough, Brougham and Pendragon, by Ranulf de Meschines, Appleby Castle changed ownership frequently between the Viponts and the Morvilles before coming into the possession of the Cliffords. The keep is mostly twelfth-century and was probably built by Henry II, who took over the castle in 1157 and again in 1173. The gatehouse was built by John Clifford in 1418 and the eastern part — hall, chapel and great chamber — by Lord Thomas Clifford in 1454. He was killed at St Albans in the Wars of the Roses.

In 1651 Lady Anne Clifford restored the castle and used it as her home. Her son-in-law, the Earl of Thanet, rebuilt the east wing with stone from Brough Castle and further repairs were done in the nineteenth century.

Open Easter to October.

Askerton

Near Kirkcambeck and Naworth, Askerton is a fortified house built by Lord Dacre on the river Cambeck. In the shape of a quadrangle, it mostly dates from the fifteenth century and was used as the base for the Land Sergeant of Liddesdale, who, under Elizabeth I, was Thomas Carleton, an opportunist who sided with the Scots if it suited him.

Askerton is a private house, not open to the public.

Bewcastle

A remote spot on a Roman site, Bewcastle is a few miles off the Brampton-Newcastleton road. The castle is a square structure with a gatehouse and one stair remaining. It had a moat but must have been easy prey to the Scots. The first owner was Giles Bueth; it then passed to the Vaux and Musgrave families; it belonged to the Grahams in the seventeenth century. In 1639 there was a garrison of a hundred men here watching the border

but Parliamentary supporters destroyed it in 1641.
Open to the public, provided permission is obtained from the farmer. Entrance is by a gate behind the farm.

Brough

William Rufus built the Norman castle on a Roman site at Brough in about 1095. It was destroyed by William the Lion of Scotland in 1174 and rebuilt by the Cliffords. Lady Anne Clifford carried out restorations in 1659-62 and her son-in-law used it as a quarry for repairing Appleby Castle in 1695.
English Heritage. Open throughout the year.

Brougham

Between Penrith and Clifton, where the river Eamont joins the Lowther, was a Roman fort called *Brocavum,* which could accommodate a thousand troops. On this site a keep was built in Henry II's reign, probably by Hugh d'Albini, and it passed to the Vipont family until the death, at the battle of Evesham, of Robert de Vipont, a supporter of Simon de Montfort. His daughter Isabella succeeded to the estate with her husband, Roger Clifford. Robert Clifford, who constructed the massive gatehouse, was killed at Bannockburn. In the seventeenth century Lady Anne Clifford, who also owned Appleby, Brough, Pendragon and Skipton castles, repaired Brougham Castle. After her death in 1676 it fell into decay once more. Her grandson Lord Tufton pulled down much of the interior and parts of it were sold in 1708 as building material.

There are Roman gravestones in a specially built museum and an old tablet to Lady Anne.
English Heritage. Open throughout the year.

Carlisle

Both the Romans and the Saxons considered Carlisle an important border stronghold, for the rock is a natural defensive position. The first castle, however, was built by William II in 1092. The Scottish king David I was responsible for building the city walls and improving the castle. For a time it was the home of the ill-fated Andrew Harcla, Earl of Carlisle, executed in 1322 for making a pact of friendship with Robert the Bruce. By 1526 the castle was much decayed and structural repairs were undertaken in 1541 by the Master of Works, Stefan von Hashenperg, known as 'The Almain', and the garrison was strengthened by eight hundred German mercenaries. Queen Elizabeth I kept Mary, Queen of Scots, at Carlisle for two months in 1568 and built a range to add to her father's half-moon battery.

During the Civil War Sir Thomas Glenham held the castle for

the king after Marston Moor. It was besieged by the Scots under Leslie and finally surrendered after Naseby, the garrison being so starved that they were reduced to eating 'rats, linseed meal and dogs'. Leslie's Scots repaired the castle with stones from the cathedral.

The most exciting episode in the long history of Carlisle was the entry of the Jacobite army in 1745. The garrison, mostly militia men, held out for seven days and then surrendered to the Duke of Perth. A small garrison was left there and on the retreat this was increased to about four hundred men under John Hamilton of Aberdeen. After a few shots at the Duke of Cumberland's army, Hamilton surrendered and the garrison was marched to London where Hamilton and another officer were hanged, drawn and quartered. After Culloden many Scots were imprisoned here and their cells can be seen in the keep.

Rebuilding occurred between 1824 and 1835, when the great parade ground was built and the new barracks replaced the great hall and the Elizabethan barracks.

English Heritage. Open throughout the year.

Clifton

This impressive peel tower is on a farm between the main road and the railway south of Penrith. It had a hall range which was taken down. Nearby is the site of the last battle on English soil, Clifton Moor (1745).

Cockermouth

Once an important castle, Cockermouth was built by William de Fortibus in the thirteenth century and was rebuilt in 1360 by Anthony de Lucy, a powerful friend of both Edward II and Edward III. It passed to the Percys and after 1585, when the eighth earl died in the Tower of London under suspicious circumstances, it fell into decay. The next owner, Charles, Duke of Somerset, repaired it and it remained virtually intact until the Civil War, when it was besieged by the Royalists and later dismantled. The outer gatehouse has a spiral staircase and the inner gatehouse was once a prison. There is an eighteenth-century building in the grounds and parts of the castle were restored during the nineteenth century.

Lord Egremont. Not open to the public.

Dacre

One of the most perfect peel towers, a few miles from Ullswater on the river Eamont, Dacre is still a family home. It was built in the thirteenth century by Ranulph Dacre, whose family built Naworth. Thomas, Lord Dacre, made some alterations to it in 1674, adding the large windows and placing his

arms over the entrance. There is a strange horseshoe-shaped moat on the lake side and twin parallel walls once ran down to the moat, so there could have been two baileys with a double wall protecting the inner one.
Open only with written permission.

Dalton-in-Furness

Near Barrow-in-Furness, Dalton is a fourteenth-century pele tower, repaired in 1544 and 1856. It has been used as a secular court for the Abbot of Furness, as a prison and as an armoury for the Rifle Volunteers.
National Trust. Open at all reasonable times. Key from 18 Market Place.

Egremont

The ford over the river Ehen at the south end of the town is commanded by the hill on which William de Meschines built his castle, one of the oldest in the county, in 1130. The vast gatehouse and herringbone curtain wall date from this period and there used to be a round keep. The great hall was on the north side and only a portion of two windows and an outer staircase remain. It belonged to the Moultons and later to the Percys but seems to have been in ruins for a long time.
Unrestricted access.

Fouldry or Piel Castle

This island fortress off Roa Island, near Barrow-in-Furness, dates from about 1327 but may have been originally a Danish outpost. It is a concentric fortress with the entrance on the west and a keep which is remarkably intact. It was repaired by the Duke of Buccleuch.

Muncaster

The Pennington family built this peel tower at Ravenglass, with outworks on the Esk estuary. During the Wars of the Roses Sir John Pennington, a Lancastrian, is said to have sheltered Henry VI, who was found wandering on the moors. The king gave Sir John an enamelled bowl, saying that the luck of Muncaster would be preserved if the bowl was kept intact. As the Penningtons still own the castle the luck has been safe-guarded. In 1826 the north-west tower was added by Salvin and Muncaster became a stately home. The gardens are renowned for azaleas and rhododendrons and the castle contains many fine paintings and furniture. It is an outstanding family home.
Mrs Patrick Gordon-Duff-Pennington. Open regularly April to September.

Naworth

Naworth is the home of the Earl of Carlisle. It can be easily seen from the Brampton to Lanercost Priory road, which goes across the park. Like many other northern castles it was originally a peel tower, built in 1335 by Ranulph de Dacre, Sheriff of Cumberland. The most famous owner was Lord Thomas Dacre, who commanded the reserves of the Earl of Surrey at Flodden in 1513. He married a ward of the king, Elizabeth of Greystoke, whom he carried off one night from neighbouring Brougham Castle.

The Dacres were involved in the rising of the northern earls against Henry VIII in 1536. Robert Aske and Lord Dacre were executed and it was not until 1603 that Lord William Dacre was restored to his property and made Warden of the Marches. He married Elizabeth, his half-sister, and was known as 'Belted Will'. The castle was restored in Tudor style and some of the panelling from nearby Kirkoswald was included in its rooms. A disastrous fire in 1844 ruined much of the castle, which was restored the following year by Salvin. The fire revealed secret chambers and a staircase. Fortunately a strong door prevented it from destroying Belted Will's tower. The Great Hall is one of the largest and finest in England.

Earl of Carlisle. Open Easter to October, Wednesdays and Sundays.

Penrith

Substantial remains of a large rectangular but unexciting castle can be seen by the railway station. It was crenellated in 1397 by William Strickland, later Bishop of Carlisle. The castle was captured by General Lambert in 1648 and used as his headquarters during the second Civil War. Never intended to be a building of active defence, Penrith Castle was built more as a shelter for the townsfolk until help could be obtained from Brougham or Carlisle.

Unrestricted access.

Sizergh

The castle of the Stricklands lies close to A6 between Kendal and Milnthorpe and is a fine example of a peel tower with a hall attached. In 1239 Elizabeth Deincourt, whose family had owned Sizergh, married Sir William Strickland. Sir Walter Strickland built the tower about 1340. His sister Jean married Robert de Wessington, ancestor of George Washington. In 1415 a Strickland carried the royal banner at Agincourt. The Stricklands were Yorkists in the Wars of the Roses and provided troops for the Earl of Salisbury. In Henry VIII's reign they were brought into court life, having intermarried in Edward IV's reign with the Parrs of Kendal. Walter Strickland was one of Elizabeth I's captains on the border. He had an armed retinue of 290 men and during his lifetime Elizabethan additions with fine panelling and alterations to the fifteenth-century Great Hall were made. Sir Robert Strickland was a Royalist and lost much of his fortune during the Civil War. Sir Thomas, his son, was a supporter of James II and followed him into exile. Many Stuart relics can be seen in a little room on the top floor.

Sir Gerald Strickland was an MP and became prime minister of Malta in 1924. He was later created Baron Strickland of Sizergh. The estate passed to his daughter and her husband, Henry Hornyold-Strickland, who, with their son, presented it to the National Trust in 1950.

National Trust. Open regularly March to October.

DERBYSHIRE

Bolsover

Just off the M1 near Chesterfield, Bolsover stands high on a rocky hill in a coal-mining area. Originally built by William Peverel in Norman times, the castle was forfeited to the Crown when his son fell from favour for poisoning the Earl of Chester. King John sent the Earl of Derby to capture Bolsover from his barons and for six years the custodian was Gerard de Furnival. The castle then passed through numerous hands until in 1613 it was sold by the Talbots to Sir Charles Cavendish, son of the Countess of Shrewsbury. The building that stands today was designed in the Jacobean Romantic style with angle towers, a central cupola and vaulted rooms. Later a long gallery was added and Sir Charles's son William, Marquis of Newcastle, built a riding school, which contains a riding display.

Charles I stayed here in 1633 before the building was completed. His entertainment, together with a masque by Ben Jonson, cost £15,000. During the Civil War the Marquis was commander-in-chief of the Royalist forces in the north and midlands. Bolsover was garrisoned but in 1644 it was taken by Major General Crawford and the Marquis fled abroad. It was slighted but partly rebuilt by young Charles Cavendish for his brother at great expense after the war.

English Heritage. Open throughout the year.

Peveril

On the A625 near Chapel-en-le-Frith, Peveril Castle, sometimes known as Peak Castle, stands in a virtually impregnable position on a rocky outcrop. William Peverel was granted the land by William the Conqueror, who had lead mines nearby.

DERBYSHIRE

Peverel had already built Bolsover Castle and was the lord of over a hundred manors in Nottinghamshire and Northampton-shire as well as Derbyshire. His son William inherited all this but lost it when his estates were forfeited in 1155 for his part in the murder of the Earl of Chester. Peveril passed to Henry II, who appointed a caretaker at the annual salary of £4 10s. The castle was much improved, especially the living quarters, and a square tower keep was erected in 1176.

Later, Peveril was owned by Simon de Montfort and by Prince Edward, and in 1310 was granted to John de Warenne, Earl of Surrey. Edward III granted it to John of Gaunt and it became a possession of the Duchy of Lancaster.

English Heritage. Open throughout the year.

DEVON

Berry Pomeroy

A few miles from Compton and to the north of the Paignton to Totnes road, the ruins of Berry Pomeroy Castle are in the middle of a dense wood. The Pomeroys came over with the Conqueror in 1066 and lived in their castle until 1549, when a riot over the reform of church services led to Sir Thomas Pomeroy leading two thousand men on Exeter. His army was defeated by Lord Russell's mercenaries and he fled. His property was confiscated by the Crown and sold to the Seymours.

Edward Seymour, Duke of Somerset, began a fine Eli-zabethan house inside the walls but never finished it. It was struck by lightning in 1685, set on fire and ruined. In spite of this, William of Orange's army camped here on their way from Torbay to London in November 1688.

Berry Pomeroy has a legend. The young Lord Berry and his cousin Genevieve were attacked by robbers while walking outside the castle. The robbers took her to a cave and she woke up to find them dead, killed by her cousin's standard-bearer, Raby Copeland. He was very badly wounded and she bound the wound with her scarf. He recovered and admitted his love for the girl. Lord Berry, who had hoped to marry Genevieve himself, gave his consent and the couple were married. Another version of the legend, however, says that he killed them both in a room in the gatehouse and that their ghosts can be seen on certain nights, trying to touch each other.

The Duke of Somerset, in the care of English Heritage. Open throughout the year.

Bickleigh

Situated on the river Exe, Bickleigh dates mostly from the fourteenth century and for many years was, like Powderham and Tiverton, one of the castles of the Courtenays, Earls of Devon.

In 1513 young Thomas Carew, who had fallen in love with the orphaned Elizabeth Courtenay, ran off with her against the family's wishes. To escape their wrath Thomas served under Lord Howard at Flodden. He fought bravely at that battle and saved the life of his commander-in-chief. He returned home to win favour at last with the Courtenays. He was given Bickleigh as Elizabeth's marriage portion. The Carews remained here for two centuries, but as they were Royalists the castle was slighted after the Civil War. Only the gatehouse and chapel seem to have escaped. These were restored in the 1920s and 1930s to form a pleasant home. Bickleigh contains fine armour, furniture and pictures.

Mr and Mrs O. N. Boxall. Open regularly Easter to October.

Compton

Off the main A381 between Newton Abbot and Totnes, Compton lies in a valley. The fortified manor, built by Geoffrey Gilbert in 1329, must be one of the few medieval manors left in its original form. In 1450 a withdrawing room was built at the west end and a small chapel next to this room at about the same period. The Great Hall was rebuilt in 1954 like the original fourteenth-century hall, with screens passage and minstrels'· gallery.

In 1520 a huge larder and kitchen were added and the 24 foot (7.3 m) high courtyard wall was built. The towers have loopholes to cover all the walls of the house.

Sir Humphrey Gilbert, Sir Walter Raleigh's half-brother, founded the British Empire by taking possession of Newfoundland. He was lost at sea on the return voyage in September 1583.

National Trust. Open April to October.

Dartmouth

This harbour fortress was originally built in 1481 by Edward IV; the Kingswear section was later added by Henry VII and once anchored a chain which stretched across to the other side in order to block the harbour. In the Civil War the town was fortified by the Royalists and there were forts called Gallant's Bower, Paradise and Mount Flaggon on one side of the river, and Kingswear fort on the other side. Tunstall church was fortified and there were batteries at Hardress and Mount Boon. In spite of this Colonel Pride and others attacked the defences in January 1646 and the governor Sir Hugh Pollare surrendered the following day.

English Heritage. Open throughout the year.

Hemyock

On the Somerset border near Wellington, stand the impressive remains of the Norman castle of the Hidons. They married into the Dynham family in the fifteenth century and Sir John Dynham was High Treasurer to Henry VII. The castle was dismantled in 1660 having been used as a prison by Parliament.
Sheppard family. Guided tours Easter to September, Sundays, Wednesdays and Bank Holidays.

Lydford

On an artificial mound within a bailey stands a square tower, believed to have been built by Richard, Earl of Cornwall, brother of Henry III. It has three rooms on one floor and above these are two others, one with a fireplace.
English Heritage. Unrestricted access.

Marisco Castle

On Lundy Island, Marisco Castle is named after a piratical family who lived there until the twelfth century. The moat and outer walls are still visible, as is the rectangular keep.
Helicopter from Hartland or boat from Bideford to Lundy.

Okehampton

The castle ruin is behind the telephone exchange on an isolated spur. Only the rectangular keep stands on an artificial motte. It belonged to the Norman Baldwin Fitzgilbert. One of his descendants was sheriff of Devon under Henry I, and from his line the Courtenays, Earls of Devon, obtained possession.

The Earl of Devon was a Lancastrian during the Wars of the Roses and twice the castle was forfeited but in 1504 Edward Courtenay defended Exeter for Henry VII against Perkin Warbeck. In 1538 Henry Courtenay, Marquis of Exeter, was involved in a plot with Cardinal Pole and Thomas Cromwell convicted him of treason. Courtenay was executed and his castle reduced to the ruin that stands today.

The main living accommodation, kitchens, gatehouse and chapel are at the bottom of the slope, isolated from the keep.
English Heritage. Open throughout the year.

Powderham

On the A379 a few miles south of Exeter, Powderham has been the home of the Courtenays for six hundred years. The castle was built by Philip, sixth son of the second Earl of Devon.

There was virtually no disturbance at Powderham until 1538, when Henry Courtenay, a cousin of Henry VIII, was imprisoned and executed the following year on a charge of treason. His son Edward was also imprisoned but was released after fourteen years by Queen Mary I and restored to his property. After he was suspected of participation in Wyatt's rebellion and he was permitted to live in Italy. During the Civil War the castle, garrisoned by Sir Hugh Meredith for the Royalists, beat off an attack in 1645 by Fairfax's troops but surrendered the following year on honourable terms. The castle escaped destruction, perhaps because Sir William Waller's daughter married a Court-enay. In the eighteenth century Powderham was turned into one of the most spectacular houses in Devon with a grand staircase decorated with elaborate plasterwork and two libraries. James Wyatt added a music room in 1790.

The Earl and Countess of Devon. For details of opening arrangements contact the Administrator, telephone Starcross (0626) 890243.

Tiverton

Next to the church remains the gatehouse of one of the largest castles in Devon. It had three round towers and one square one and a wide double moat. It fell into decay in Tudor times after its owner, the Marquis of Exeter, was executed for treason by Henry VIII. During the Civil War it was garrisoned by three hundred Royalists but General Massey captured it after a lucky shot broke the drawbridge chain and exposed the inner courtyard. The remains of a fourteenth-century hall and chapel are also visible. Tiverton houses an interesting clock collection, French, Italian and English furnishings and has a Restoration wing open on special occasions.

Mr and Mrs A. K. Gordon. Open regularly Easter to September.

Totnes

A shell-keep similar to Launceston (Cornwall), Totnes was never of great military importance. Built by the Nonants in the eleventh century, it passed to the Zouche family. In later days it was used as a prison. There used to be a square tower in the keep and a second bailey was constructed for cattle on the outside of the moat to the north. The structure is in excellent condition.

English Heritage. Open throughout the year.

DORSET

Brownsea

On an island in Poole Harbour Henry VIII had a defensive blockhouse, which was used by Sir Christopher Hatton to extract money from passing ships. It was mostly burnt down in 1895.

National Trust. Open April to September. Boats from Sandbanks and Poole Quay.

Christchurch

The castle mound and remains of the keep stand near the abbey on high ground once surrounded by a rectangular moat connected to the Avon. It was built by Richard de Redvers, Earl of Devon, and his son during the reign of Henry I and was captured by Walter de Pinkney in 1147. In the grounds belonging to the local bowling club stands the constable's house, dating from about 1160. It has the remains of a water gate and a remarkable chimney and flue, which make it appear entirely separate from the rugged remains of the keep.

English Heritage. Unrestricted access to the keep.

Corfe

One of the noblest and best known ruins in England, Corfe Castle stands high up in a gap in the Purbeck Hills. The first building was probably erected by King Edgar, whose son Edward was murdered here in 978. His stepmother is said to have had him stabbed.

The Duke of Brittany and several French captives were imprisoned here by King John and twenty-two starved to death in a dungeon. Henry III turned it into a royal palace and Edward II spent a night here on his last journey to Berkeley. The ill-starred Duke of Clarence owned it during the reign of Edward IV, and the Protector Somerset until his execution for treason in 1552. In Elizabethan times the Hattons owned it and in 1635 it was sold to Sir John Bankes. He was with Charles I when the Parliamentary forces from Poole attacked Corfe, which was defended by his wife and their small garrison. Two attacks were beaten off but in 1646 a Colonel Pitman turned traitor and admitted the enemy, forcing Lady Bankes to surrender. The slighting was very thorough and one of the gatehouse towers was split in two. The wall between the gatehouse and keep remains.

National Trust. Open throughout the year (weekends only in winter).

Portland

Henry VIII built a coastal fort here and at Weymouth, Sandsfoot (now destroyed), to command Weymouth and protect Portland Harbour. It was manned at the time of the Armada. It was captured by Royalists during the Civil War and held until April 1646. The whole of Portland was a fortress in the Second World War and ports of the fort still look as if the guns had only recently been removed.

English Heritage. Open April to September.

Rufus Castle

Overlooking Church Ope Cove on the east coast of Portland Bill are the remains of William Rufus's castle. It has a round gun port overlooking the blocked-up bridge. It is also known as Bow and Arrow Castle. Nearby is Portland Museum.

Sherborne (Old Castle)

Roger de Caen's building at Sherborne is well situated on a commanding hill with steep ground to the north and west and a wide moat on the other two sides. Roger, Bishop of Salisbury, was Regent to Henry I during the king's frequent journeys abroad. He also built Devizes, Old Sarum and Malmesbury castles. In 1139 Roger was imprisoned by Stephen for his friendship with Matilda. His castle fell into decay and subsequently had several owners, including Lord Somerset, until Elizabeth I presented it to Sir Walter Raleigh. He, however, decided that it was too decayed and built the new castle nearby.

There were three gateways to Sherborne: the north, with its long vaulted passage, which has been completely restored; the north-east is completely ruined; the south-west is the best preserved. The main buildings are in the centre, with the great hall on the ground floor and the chapel on the first floor. There is a large Norman pillar supporting a bay window which faces south, an alteration dating from the sixteenth century. In James I's reign the Earl of Somerset was sent to the Tower for his part in the murder of Sir Thomas Overbury and the castle passed to Baron Digby, former ambassador to Madrid. His descendants, the Wingfield-Digbys, own the land today.

During the Civil War the castle was garrisoned for the king and was besieged twice. In 1642 the Parliamentarians were driven off and in 1645 there was a fifteen-day siege in which the Portsmouth siege train had to be brought up to batter down the walls before Sir Lewis Dives surrendered.

English Heritage. Open throughout the year.

DURHAM

Auckland

The castle at Bishop Auckland is still the home of the Bishop of Durham. It was built by Bishop Bec and rebuilt by Wyatt and has a great hall, now the chapel, and a fine wood-panelled private chapel off the throne room. It once had a stone curtain wall. In the grounds stands an eighteenth-century deer shelter, somewhat similar to that at Sudbury in Derbyshire.

Open on Wednesdays and Sundays, May to September.

Barnard Castle

Barnard Castle was built on the Tees in 1130 by Bernard Balliol. (The site had been given to Guy Balliol of Bailleul by William Rufus.) The next owner, Hugh Balliol, was a favourite of King John. During the Barons' War in 1216 the castle was besieged but one of Hugh's men killed the Lord of Alnwick, who was fighting for the Scots, with a shot from his crossbow, and the attackers retreated. After passing to the Nevilles, the castle came to Charles, Earl of Westmorland, who was one of the supporters of Mary, Queen of Scots, during the Rising of the North in 1569. He was forced to flee the country after trying unsuccessfully to drive out Sir George Bowes, who in his absence had captured Barnard Castle for Elizabeth I. The Crown confiscated the property, leasing it to various people including the Vanes. This family held the castle for the Royalists during the Civil War, when it was badly damaged by Parliamentary cannon and captured.

There are four baileys, the large outer and town baileys and the smaller middle and inner ones. The main keep, Baliol Tower, was so strongly built that at one time it was used as a shot tower, thereby damaging its vaulting and floor.

English Heritage. Open throughout the year.

Bowes

Not far from Barnard Castle, Bowes stands on the Roman site of *Lavatrae,* commanding the road from York to Appleby. The castle was built between 1170 and 1187 by the Earl of Richmond and consists of a large square Norman keep, although it once had two baileys.

English Heritage. Open throughout the year.

Brancepeth

A few miles south-west of Durham is Brancepeth Castle, built by the Bulmers before 1100 and inherited by the Nevilles in 1174. Today it is mostly eighteenth- and nineteenth-century work that stands but parts remain of Ralph Neville's fourteenth-century castle. Ralph, grandfather of Warwick the Kingmaker, was Marshal of England from 1399 to 1425.

In 1569 the sixth Earl of Westmorland fought in the Rising of the North and the property was confiscated by the Crown. It was owned for a time by the Earl of Somerset and in 1701 was bought by Sir Henry Belasyse. In 1796 William Russell, a Sunderland banker, bought it and, with his son Matthew, the richest commoner in England, spent more than £120,000 restoring it. The work was carried out by an Edinburgh architect called Patterson who had a fondness for Norman work but not very much imagination.

Mr and Mrs Dobson. Not open to the public.

Durham

Standing inside an incised meander of the river Wear, Durham Castle makes a handsome partner to the great cathedral. It was a Norman stronghold and the original castle was built by William I about 1072. It was strengthened and enlarged by Bishop Pudsey in 1174. The present entrance has massive sixteenth-century doors, which lead into a courtyard. Bishop Bec's Great Hall is on the left. It has a large collection of paintings and armour and has seen many famous guests, including Sir Walter Scott and the Duke of Wellington. The kitchen was once a guardroom. Above is Bishop Pudsey's Norman doorway; to reach it one goes up the Black Staircase, installed in 1663 by Bishop Cosin. The Senate Room has a sixteenth-century tapestry and underneath is a small chapel, dating from 1070, the oldest room in the castle. A new chapel was built nearby in 1542 with fittings from Auckland Castle. The massive keep was converted into rooms for students in 1840 and the castle is now University College.
Open throughout the year.

Raby

At Staindrop on the main A688 road between Bishop Auckland and Barnard Castle, Raby is one of the finest fourteenth-century castles in England. Sir John Nevill, who as a boy had seen his father victorious at Neville's Cross, obtained a licence to crenellate his home in 1378. He was High Admiral of England and his son Ralph, the first Earl of Westmorland, may have fought at Agincourt. His first wife was Margaret, daughter of Hugh, Earl of Stafford; his second was Joan Beaufort, John of Gaunt's daughter. He had twenty-one children by his two wives and the youngest of them, Cicely, was known as the 'Rose of Raby'. She married Richard Plantagenet, Duke of York, and was the mother of Edward IV and Richard III. The sixth Earl, Charles, was the last Nevill to bear the title of Westmorland; he escaped abroad following the Rising in the North in 1569 and later died in Holland. Raby was forfeited to the Crown.

In 1626 it was purchased by Sir Henry Vane. The Vanes were Parliamentarians during the Civil War and, although the Royalists from Bolton captured it in 1645, Sir Henry's son George retook it before it suffered any damage. In 1698 Christopher Vane was created the first Lord Barnard and in 1714, attempting to injure the inheritance of his son, who had married against his wishes, he stripped the lead off the castle's roof and attempted to pull down the walls. Luckily the law intervened and Raby was saved. The south facade was altered by the architect Burn in 1840 but it was done in such a way that the effect of the castle from a distance is dramatic.

Lord Barnard TD. Open Easter to September. Picnic area, gardens and carriage museum also open.

EAST SUSSEX

Bodiam

Situated just off the A229 Hastings to Hawkhurst road, Bodiam was built in 1386-8 by Sir Edward Dalyngrigge to protect the river Rother from French raiding parties which frequently attacked the coast at Rye and Winchelsea. During the wars in France, Dalyngrigge had made a fortune. His wife was the heiress of the Wardeux family which owned Bodiam and by the terms of the licence dated 21st October 1385 he was entitled to 'strengthen his manor house with a wall of stone and lime'. The castle is rectangular with a wide moat and two entrances, the main one having two drawbridges and a fortified bridge head.

Within defensive range of the castle a harbour was built for ships sailing up the Rother. In 1483, during the reign of Richard III, Bodiam was held for Henry Tudor by one of the Lewknors. He was attainted and the Earl of Surrey was ordered to take the castle. No damage appears to have been done at that time. It was reduced to ruin by Sir William Waller after his capture of Arundel in 1643. The later owners were Tuftons, Powells, Websters, Fullers and Cubitts and in 1917, Lord Curzon, who restored it.

National Trust. Open throughout the year.

Camber

Camber Castle, 1½ miles (2.4 km) south-east of Rye, was built in 1539-40 by Henry VIII for coastal defence. It was one of the first 'modern' fortifications designed to make full use of cannon, in this anticipating the Napoleonic fortifications of 250 years later. It was dismantled in 1642, when abandoned by the sea, which is now a mile (1.6 km) away.

English Heritage. Closed to the public while undergoing repairs.

Hastings

The site of the original castle at Hastings is now under the sea. The ruins seen today are mostly of the chapel of St Mary and date from the thirteenth century. In about 1069 Robert, Count of Eu, was granted this land, William the Conqueror's first English possession, and replaced the king's wooden castle, brought over from Normandy as depicted in the Bayeux Tapestry, with a stone one. The castle was often held by the Crown. The last owners were the Pelhams and today it stands in a small park. There are two underground 'dungeons' of unusual interest.

Hastings Borough Council. Open mid April to mid September.

Herstmonceux

One of the most remarkable and least accessible castles in England, Herstmonceux lies in a valley off A271 between Lewes and Battle. It was originally a Norman manor of Robert, Earl of Eu, and later (about 1200) belonging to the Herst family from Monceux, near Bayeux in Normandy. Their last heiress married Sir John de Fiennes in 1320 and her great-grandson, Sir Roger, obtained a licence in 1441 and built the castle. He was a veteran of Agincourt, Treasurer of the Household to Henry VI, and became Lord Dacre. Of a similar age to Tattershall (Lincolnshire), Herstmonceux was also built of bricks. There were four courts: a large Green Court, a smaller Pump Court, a tiny Chicken Court and one other; also there was a strange chamber known as Drummer's Hall, where it is said a French gardener used to beat a drum to distract the family's attention from smugglers.

The Dacres lived here until the end of Elizabeth I's reign, when the castle passed to the Leonards, who assumed the title of Dacre. A Dacre married the illegitimate daughter of Charles II and the Duchess of Cleveland but his extravagance forced him to sell the castle to George Naylor for £38,215. Mr Naylor died without issue and the castle passed to Dr Hare, Bishop of Chichester, whose second son, Robert, was responsible in 1777 for commissioning Samuel Wyatt to build nearby Herstmonceux Place out of much of the interior brick of the castle. The tapestries, furniture and sculptures were all auctioned. The castle remained a ruin until Colonel Claude Lowther rebuilt it with one courtyard in 1913 and it was further restored by Sir Paul Latham in 1933.

Royal Observatory. The gardens and two rooms with displays on the history of the castle and of astronomy are open from Easter to September.

Lewes

Earl William de Warenne began building the first castle at Lewes in the late eleventh century. During the fourteenth century it passed to Richard Fitzalan, thirteenth Earl of Arundel, who was the son of Alice, the sister of the last Earl Warenne. It is unique in having two mottes. An elliptical shell-keep was raised on the western mound; the projecting polygonal towers, of which two remain, were added in the thirteenth century. The fine Barbican, or outer gatehouse, was erected in the fourteenth century.

John, the seventh Earl, fought under Henry III at the battle of Lewes in 1264, fleeing to France on defeat. The following year he returned and took part in the battle at Evesham.

In the castle grounds are interpretative displays, iron railings made in Sussex for St Paul's Cathedral, a Russian gun of the Crimean War, two prehistoric canoes and other interesting items. In Barbican House, opposite the castle entrance, is a museum housing the archaeology collections of the Sussex Archaeological Society.
Sussex Archaeological Society. Open throughout the year.

Pevensey
Pevensey Castle once stood beside the sea but with the gradual alteration of the coast line, it now lies about a mile inland on A259 between Eastbourne and Bexhill. One of the nine Saxon Shore forts, Pevensey was the Roman *Anderida*. It is an oval of 10 acres (4 ha) surrounded by most of the original Roman walls. The Normans landed near here and there is a small monument to William the Conqueror by the main gate. The Norman castle was built about 1100 by Count Robert of Mortain and his son William and strengthened with stone walls, a keep and a water-filled moat in the thirteenth century. The keep uses the east wall of the Roman fort for its outer wall. The main entrance was from the west gate, but the visitor now enters by the east gate, which once probably led to the harbour. Inside the keep are some interesting ballista missiles, a dungeon, an oubliette, remains of a chapel and an Elizabethan cannon probably used to defend the castle during the Armada alert.
Pevensey has several times been besieged. In 1088, after the death of the Conqueror, Bishop Odo supported the claims of Robert, the Conqueror's brother, against William Rufus, who besieged the castle until it was starved into surrender. In 1147 the castle was besieged by Stephen and again the hungry garrison, under the Earl of Clare, was forced to surrender. It withstood a siege by Simon de Montfort the younger and another in the fourteenth century when Lady Pelham, in her husband's absence, held out for Henry Bolingbroke against Richard II. It was then held by the Crown until bestowed by William III on the Bentincks, who sold it to the Earl of Wilmington, from whom it passed in 1782 to the Dukes of Devonshire. After this it was used as a quarry and decayed into ruin. During the Second World War, however, it was fitted with several ingenious machine-gun positions, the one on the north-west bastion looking like part of the Norman building. Observation troops and the US Army Air Corps were residents as well as Canadians and the Home Guard. The west gate was fitted with a blockhouse containing anti-tank weapons and a new tower was added to the eastern wall. In 1945 it was restored and the blockhouse was removed.
English Heritage. Open throughout the year.

1. *Donnington Castle, Berkshire.*

2. *Restormel Castle, Cornwall.*

3. St Mawes Castle, Cornwall, with Pendennis Castle visible in the distance.

4. Tintagel Castle, Cornwall.

5. *Peveril Castle, Derbyshire.*

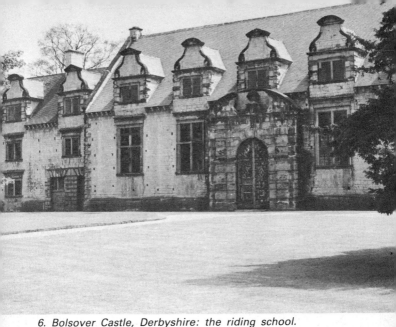

6. Bolsover Castle, Derbyshire: the riding school.
7. Hastings Castle, East Sussex.

8. Lewes Castle, East Sussex.

9. Colchester Castle, Essex.

10. Berkeley Castle, Gloucestershire.

11. Hurst Castle, Hampshire.

12. Goodrich Castle, Hereford and Worcester.

13. Canterbury Castle, Kent.

14. Tonbridge Castle, Kent.

15. *Walmer Castle, Kent.*

16. *Clitheroe Castle, Lancashire.*

17. Kirby Muxloe Castle, Leicestershire.

18. South Kyme Tower, Lincolnshire.

19. *Norwich Castle, Norfolk.*

20. *Alnwick Castle, Northumberland.*

21. Bamburgh Castle, Northumberland.
22. Dunstanburgh Castle, Northumberland.

23. Warkworth Castle, Northumberland.
24. Middleham Castle, North Yorkshire.

25. Richmond Castle, North Yorkshire.

26. Scarborough Castle, North Yorkshire.

27. Pickering Castle, North Yorkshire.

28. Newark Castle, Nottinghamshire.

29. Minister Lovell Hall, Oxfordshire.

ESSEX

Colchester

Colchester Castle was begun in the reign of William I on the site of a Roman temple. The rectangular keep, the largest in England, was surrounded by a ditch and rampart covering the walls of the temple court. The outer bailey extended to the walls north of the town. The keep was fortified with battlements on its first floor, but two more storeys were added later. The north entrance, reconstructed in the early twelfth century, was later protected by outbuildings.

The massive ruin was roofed over and fitted with galleries in 1932. On the first floor are four enormous fireplaces with bricks laid in herringbone pattern. There was a chapel on the second floor in the south-east corner, similar to that in the White Tower of the Tower of London. The similarity between the two castles suggests that they were designed by the same man.

The history of the castle is the history of Colchester. It was granted to Eudo, steward to William I and Henry I, and on his death it reverted to the Crown. Hamo St Clare was constable in the twelfth century and later this office passed to William de Lanvalai. King John distrusted the third generation de Lanvalai and replaced him with a Fleming, Stephen Harengoot, who fortified the castle with two 24 inch (610 mm) and six 12 inch (305 mm) ballistas from London. In 1215 seven thousand men landed in Suffolk from France and a force under the Earl of Winchester, including many French soldiers, occupied the castle. It was attacked by Savaric de Mauleon and King John. The French fought furiously, using the ballistas, but were defeated and once more Harengoot was installed as constable.

Shortly after this the keep was used as a prison, but during the Civil War the Royalists held Colchester for three months against Fairfax and the New Model Army. After a twelve-week siege the town finally surrendered in August 1648. Sir Charles Lucas and Sir George Lisle, two of the leaders of the revolt, were, according to tradition, imprisoned in the long vault near the wellhouse until, as an example to others, they were taken outside to face the Parliamentary firing squad. Sir Charles Lucas was shot first and Lisle ran over to pay his respects before he too faced the firing squad. Today a stone outside the castle keep marks the spot where they died.

The structure was partly pulled down in 1683 by a local ironmonger, who happily found the task too great and soon gave it up. Colchester Castle is now the Colchester and Essex Museum. It contains an extensive archaeological collection, including some of the best Roman remains in Britain.
Colchester Borough Council. Open throughout the year.

Hadleigh

In south Essex, not far from Leigh-on-Sea, stand the remains of Hadleigh Castle on a hill overlooking the Thames estuary. It was built by Hubert de Burgh, Chief Justiciar of King John and Henry III, of Kentish stone ferried across the river and up a creek that has since silted up. Henry VIII's 'Flanders Mare', Anne of Cleves, who 'spoke only German and spent her time chiefly in needlework', lived here after her divorce.

The castle, made famous by John Constable's painting, differs from the usual medieval design in having no keep. The entrance was at the north, protected by a barbican adjacent to a large tower which may have acted as the keep, protected by a drawbridge and portcullis. The main offices were to the south-west, where there were timber buildings against the wall and a circular tower with a dungeon.

English Heritage. Open throughout the year.

Hedingham Castle

Castle Hedingham is a charming village dominated by the Castle with its splendid Norman keep similar to but smaller than that at Rochester in Kent.

The de Vere family, who built it in 1130, were frequently at war. Robert, second Earl of Oxford, fought against King John, who laid siege to the castle in 1216. The following year it was besieged by the Dauphin. Robert de Vere's son fought for Simon de Montfort at Lewes and another de Vere, the seventh Earl of Oxford, fought at Crecy. The ninth Earl was a favourite of Richard II and married Edward III's granddaughter. He was created a marquis, the first in England.

A famous Earl of Oxford was the Lancastrian soldier who fought with Warwick at the battle of Barnet. He was imprisoned for many years by the Yorkists in France but escaped and in 1485 landed with Henry Tudor, commanding his vanguard at Bosworth Field.

The banqueting hall, has a minstrel's gallery and an extremely fine Norman arch. The drawbridge was replaced in 1496 by the Tudor bridge which still spans the dry moat. In 1713 the castle passed to the Trentham family, then to the Ashursts, one of whom built the house in the outer bailey, and to their relatives, the Majendies, whose successor, the present owner, happens to be a descendant of the de Veres.

The Hon. Thomas and Mrs Lindsay. Open May to September.

Pleshey

Originally a motte and bailey castle of the twelfth century, Pleshey still has a motte 50 feet (15 m) high, a moat crossed by a fifteenth-century bridge and a huge outer bailey that encloses most of the village. Geoffrey de Mandeville, owner of Saffron Walden Castle, was the first known owner of Pleshey. He surrendered it to King Stephen in 1142. It was ordered to be destroyed in 1157 but was refortified 1167-80. It passed to the Bohuns, Earls of Hereford. Eleanor de Bohun was the wife of the Duke of Gloucester, uncle of Richard II. The Duke tried to rule the young king and opposed the marriage of his own brother's son to his wife's younger sister Mary de Bohun. Richard set out with a party of soldiers for Pleshey and enticed the Duke away. On their way back to London the party was ambushed and the Duke was carried off to Calais on Richard's orders. The unfortunate man was later strangled and brought back to Pleshey to be buried next to his wife. His family got their revenge three years later when the Duke of Exeter, who had been responsible for the ambush, was beheaded by a mob outside the castle walls.

In 1629 Robert Clarke, the then owner, pulled down most of the castle to build a house called the Lodge. This was later sold to Sir William Joliffe, whose monument can be seen in the church. There is a stone from the castle in the churchyard which has on it the name 'Richard II' inscribed in Latin.
Unrestricted access.

Saffron Walden

Little remains of this castle. In Church Street are the flint walls of the keep dating from the eleventh or twelfth centuries. There used to be another building west of the keep, reached by a staircase. At the time of Domesday the manor belonged to Geoffrey de Mandeville, who probably built the castle. His grandson, also Geoffrey, fought for Queen Matilda against King Stephen and had to forfeit Saffron Walden, together with Pleshey Castle and his position as Constable of the Tower of London. He was later killed by an arrow while attacking Burwell Castle near Cambridge.

Later the castle passed to his niece Beatrix de Saye, wife of the Chief Justice of England and a friend of King John. When they died the property passed to their daughter Maud, wife of the Earl of Hereford, Lord High Constable of England. In 1347 Maud's son Humphrey obtained a licence to crenellate what must have been mainly a domestic building. On his death it reverted to the Crown and became part of the Duchy of Lancaster. Henry VIII presented it to the Lords Audley and from this family it descended to the Howards, Earls of Suffolk.

GLOUCESTERSHIRE

Berkeley

The building of the present castle was begun by Roger de Berkeley in 1117 and completed by his son, also Roger, in about 1153. The castle was granted to Robert FitzHarding, who was created Baron Berkeley, following the younger Roger's opposition to Henry II. The Berkeleys opposed King John and later joined Simon de Montfort's rebellion. In spite of this they continued to hold their property, mainly because of Thomas Berkeley, who fought valiantly for Edward I in his northern campaign.

When Edward II was deposed by Queen Isabella and Roger Mortimer, Thomas Berkeley was turned out of his castle, which was used as a prison for the king under two guardians, Lord Maltravers and Thomas Gurney. One of the cruellest deeds in English history took place on 21st September 1327 when the king was murdered in the castle. Thomas Berkeley was exonerated from any complicity in the murder and young Edward III soon had his revenge on Mortimer (*see* Nottingham Castle).

Thomas's grandson was one of Henry Bolingbroke's supporters in the deposition of Richard II and when he died in 1417 the ownership of the castle and estate was disputed between his son-in-law and his nephew James Berkeley. The latter was awarded the estate but during the Wars of the Roses Thomas's daughter's grandson Lord Lisle and James's son William waged a private war that had no connection with the major war that was going on elsewhere in England. In 1470 at the battle of Nibley Green Lisle was defeated and killed. William had no heirs and rather than recognise any of his cousins he granted the castle to Henry VII in exchange for the title of Earl Marshal in 1486. For sixty-one years the castle was held by the Crown until the great grandson of William's brother Maurice inherited it on the death of Edward VI.

During the Civil War Berkeley Castle was occupied by both sides and finally the Royalist Sir Charles Lucas surrendered to Colonel Rainsborough in 1645 after a three-day siege. The usual slighting was not attempted as Berkeley was popular with both sides. Only the outer wall was demolished and the keep breached, as it remains still. In 1679 George Berkeley was made an earl but owing to a complication in inheritance in 1810 the

'Berkeley Peerage Case' left the castle in different hands for a hundred years until the earls once again possessed it in 1916.

The Norman shell-keep has been flattened on the top to give more space. This leads out to the inner ward, where there is the chapel, the great hall built during the reign of Edward III and the residential quarters, all somewhat similar to an Oxford or Cambridge college. Edward II's prison was in one of the three semicircular keep towers although he is believed to have been murdered in a room above the forebuilding, described by Horace Walpole as 'a dismal chamber in a square tower'.

Mr and Mrs R. J. Berkeley. Open April to October.

St Briavels

At St Briavels on the B4228, north-east of Chepstow, stands the small twelfth-century castle of Milo Fitzwalter. It consists of a massive gatehouse and kitchen, the keep having fallen down in the eighteenth century. Most of the present structure dates from the reign of Edward I but during the reign of King John the castle was used as a hunting residence. Apparently Milo's son, Mahel, who was 'cruel and covetous', entertained Walter de Clifford here and a small fire in the castle brought down a stone on Mahel's head which killed him. The old chapel, which was made into a court room, was converted back into a chapel at a later date.

Not open to the public.

Sudeley

The fortified manor of Sudeley near Winchcombe, off the A46, is famous as the last resting place of Queen Catharine Parr, who was the sixth wife of Henry VIII and survived him. The building that stands today was designed by Sir John Soane and later by Sir Giles Gilbert Scott.

Catharine Parr married Thomas Seymour after the death of Henry VIII, and he was presented with Sudeley. In 1549 he was put to death by Somerset and Catharine's brother William took possession of the property until his execution for participation in Wyatt's revolt in 1554. The next owner, Sir John Brydges, Earl of Chandos, was a supporter of Queen Mary I and his son later became Constable of the Tower, a duty which he exercised with great tact: Queen Mary ordered Princess Elizabeth to be executed but young Brydges delayed the warrant and saved her life.

George Brydges, sixth Earl of Chandos, was an ardent Royalist and raised his own regiment to fight for Charles I.

Unfortunately during his absence on New Year's Day 1642, Colonel Massey arrived from Gloucester and set fire to some outbuildings, capturing the castle under cover of the smoke. Lord Chandos returned in 1643 and recaptured it but did not hold it for long and for many years it was a ruin. In 1837 John and William Dent of Worcester restored part of it with care and Catharine's tomb, which had been broken open in 1782, was with its chapel made into 'a most exquisite gem of ecclesiastical architecture'.

The Lady Ashcombe. Open April to October.

GREATER LONDON

Tower of London

The building of the White Tower or keep was probably begun by William I in 1078, on the site of the original ditch and palisade set inside the old city wall. Strangely, the sides of the White Tower are not regular and three corners are not right angles. At ground level the walls are 15 feet (4.6 m) thick. The White Tower marked the eastern flank of the structure and the ruined Wardrobe Tower forms the half-way point in the east wall, which ran from the Bowyer Tower to the Lanthorn Tower. In the thirteenth century the castle was enlarged to its present size of 18 acres (7.3 ha) and today it contains examples of many periods of architecture.

The Tower was a royal palace until the reign of James I. The palace buildings were situated between the White Tower and the Inner Wall, east of the Bloody Tower. Many famous prisoners have been kept in the White Tower and in the Queen's House, among them Robert Dudley, Earl of Essex, Sir Walter Raleigh, Judge Jeffreys, the Duke of Monmouth, Lord Nithsdale, Sir Roger Casement and Rudolf Hess. In the White Tower is the Chapel of St John, which was restored by Wren. On the south side of the tower two children's skeletons were discovered during the reign of Charles II. They were supposed to have been those of the two princes, sons of Edward IV, who vanished during the reign of Richard III and whose murder remains a mystery.

For the visitor, the two main attractions of the Tower are the Crown Jewels and the Armouries. The jewels date mostly from the seventeenth century as most of the original ones were broken up by the Parliamentarians after the Civil War. The only older pieces are the Anointing Spoon, of the twelfth century, and the eagle-shaped Ampulla, which dates from Henry IV's reign. Both St Edward's Crown, made for Charles II's coronation, and the Imperial State Crown, made in 1838, are on display. The

Armouries contain weapons and armour from Henry VIII's reign to the present day. Small arms are kept on the ground floor and swords and daggers on the first floor. On the top floor are personal weapons of the kings of England. The Mortar Room has an interesting collection, including a gun from the *Royal George*, sunk by accident in Portsmouth Harbour in 1782.

The Royal Fusiliers have a special museum containing three Victoria Crosses won by the regiment and models of the battles of Albuera, Alma, Mons and Monte Cassino. In the Royal Chapel of St Peter ad Vincula are buried the remains of the prisoners executed at the Tower, the last three being Scottish lords beheaded in 1747 for their part in the Jacobite Rising. On Tower Green scaffolds were erected for the execution of two of Henry VIII's wives, Anne Boleyn and Catharine Howard, as well as Lord Hastings, Lady Jane Grey, Margaret Countess of Salisbury, Jane Viscountess Rochford, and Elizabeth I's Essex.

In 1673 the Martin Tower was the scene of a desperate attempt to steal the Crown Jewels by a Hampshire soldier, Colonel Blood. Hiding the crown in his cloak and the orb in his pocket, the Colonel and his accomplices attempted to file the sceptre in half to conceal it. Colonel Blood was pardoned by Charles II, who gave him a pension and some Irish estates.

Among various ceremonies associated with the Tower is the Ceremony of the Keys, which takes place at 10 p.m. every night. The Chief Warder and his escort close the gates. By the Bloody Tower there is the guard's customary challenge, to which the Chief Warder replies, ending with the salute 'God preserve Queen Elizabeth' and the sentry's response 'Amen', before the keys are taken to the Queen's House for the night. Royal salutes are fired from the Tower by a detachment of the Honourable Artillery Company and there is an impressive ceremony on the installation of a new Governor. The famous ravens are kept in a cage by the Lanthorn Tower and given a weekly allocation of horseflesh.

English Heritage. Open throughout the year.

HAMPSHIRE

Basing House

A fortified house constructed on the site of a thirteenth-century ringwork and bailey, Basing is renowned for its defence during the Civil War by the Royalist Marquess of Winchester. The Paulets added a fifteenth-century crenellated house, of which only the gatehouse, a few walls and the remains of the keep stand today. During the famous three-year siege, which ended in a bloody fight on 14th October 1645, some two thousand Parliamentarians lost their lives. The castle was completely demolished and the Marquess and Inigo Jones, the

distinguished architect, were taken prisoner with a few other survivors. There is a small museum and a gatehouse and a dovecote remain, together with a secret tunnel.
Open Easter to September.

Bishop's Waltham

About 1135 Bishop Henry of Blois built here a moated residence, which was converted into a palace by William of Wykeham. Fortified by the Royalists during the Civil War, it was captured in 1645, the Bishop of Winchester escaping in a dung cart, and the castle was demolished.
English Heritage. Open throughout the year.

Calshot

A small blockhouse erected at the time of Henry VIII, Calshot was constructed to defend the entrance to Southampton harbour. It has a round tower and platform with a surrounding gun terrace and embrasures. There is an exhibition.
English Heritage. Open Easter to September.

Hurst

Near Milford-on-Sea, Hurst Castle is situated at the end of a 2 mile (3 km) stretch of shingle facing the Isle of Wight. It dates from Henry VIII's reign, when similar castles were also built at Southsea, Netley and Calshot, but Hurst is the most extensive of the four. It originally consisted of a central twelve-sided tower with a curtain wall, and three large semicircular bastions containing unusual eyebrow gunports. Until the seventeenth century the castle was not well maintained and only in 1635 was it equipped with iron guns in place of the brass ones. During the Civil War it was held for Parliament and Charles I was brought here from Carisbrooke shortly before his execution. He arrived on 29th November 1648 by boat and left on 18th December escorted by Colonel Harrison. His room at the castle on the second floor was only 8 by 4½ feet (2.4 by 1.4 m).

During the years following the Restoration thirty guns were installed and in the eighteenth century the castle was used as a prison. In 1861 the entire castle was enlarged and built round so that only from the inside today is it possible to realise the size of the original building. There is a narrow-gauge rail network built for transporting shells for the naval guns, and Hurst is the only English castle with a railway running over its drawbridge. There is an ingenious lift from the basement magazine for lifting shells to the ground floor. During the First World War heavy coastal artillery was installed, and the tracks and mooring stanchions are still in place. The entrance in the north-west bastion is protected by a caponiere built in the nineteenth century for covering the moat with musket fire should an attempt be made to capture the castle from the land side.

English Heritage. Open throughout the year. Take the ferry from Keyhaven or walk at low tide (about 35 minutes).

Odiham

King John's castle, in which a gallant force of thirteen men held out for two weeks in 1216 against the French, is on the canal at North Warnborough. Part of the keep remains and is noted as the only octagonal keep in the country.

Unrestricted access.

Portchester

This is probably the best surviving Roman fort in England. It was square and covered 9 acres (3.6 ha) but after the Romans abandoned Portchester it was not inhabited again until an Augustinian priory was established in 1133 in the south-east corner of the square. At about that time Henry I built the stone keep in the opposite corner. The top two storeys of the tower were added later, together with the inner ward.

Portchester played an important part in history because the fleet could shelter beneath its walls. It was held by Simon de Montfort for a time, and from here Henry V set sail on his Agincourt campaign. Henry VI's queen, Margaret of Anjou, arrived at Portchester from France and Elizabeth I often used it.

During the Napoleonic Wars it became a prison and at one time there were four thousand men here. There is a story that a senior officer left his horse at the gate while he was seeing the governor and returned a few hours later to find that the French prisoners, who were always short of food, had stolen and eaten the animal.

The inner ward was protected by its own drawbridge with a 15 foot (4.6 m) long passage somewhat similar to that at Prudhoe (Northumberland). The water gate of two storeys was built by the Romans but has been repaired on several occasions.

English Heritage. Open throughout the year.

Portsmouth

In 1848 the downfall of the French monarchy and the advent of Napoleon III caused general alarm in England. Lord Palmerston set about building a series of forts to protect the fleet at Portsmouth, which had by then become a naval port more important than Chatham. An outer line of forts protecting Gosport was planned but only Fort Fareham, now used as a store, was built. An inner line extended from Fort Gomer near Alverstoke to Fort Elson, with Fort Grange (now a Royal Navy building), Fort Rowner (Royal Navy) and Fort Brockhurst in between. The forts are very solidly constructed with caponieres (covered passages) and underground barracks with fireplaces. The ramparts are equipped for both guns and rifles and built of granite as well as brick. To prevent an encircling movement and an attack from the north, Palmerston placed six forts on Portsdown Hill. These are Fort Wallington at Fareham, Fort Nelson, Fort Southwick, Fort Widley, Fort Purbrook and Farlington Redoubt.

Fort Brockhurst (English Heritage), open April to September. Fort Widley (Portsmouth City Council), open April to September, weekends only. Fort Nelson (Hampshire County Council), open April to September, weekends only.

Southampton

Part of the bailey wall still remains on Western Esplanade. Once a wooden structure, it was the centre of the walled town that was stormed by the French in 1338. Sir John Arundel repaired it and in 1377 it held out against a further French attack. A block of flats has been built on the site of Lord Stafford's banqueting hall. The castle had a water gate and vault which still remain, and the bailey covered 3 acres (1.2 ha). The eastern gate has been uncovered and restored. The town walls are, with those of Berwick-upon-Tweed, the best surviving in England.

Southsea

One of the most interesting Hampshire castles, Southsea was built in 1543-4 by Henry VIII; it comprises a square keep within a diamond. It was restored and strengthened in 1814 by Major General Fisher of the Royal Engineers, who also enlarged it to accommodate his two hundred men and some 32 pound (14.5 kg) cannon, but none of the original ones are on display. The Tudor gun ports are also visible and at one time the roof of the keep supported four traversing guns fed by ammunition hoists in the roofs of the first-floor galleries.

In 1642 the governor, Captain Challoner, holding the castle for the king in support of Colonel Goring in Portsmouth, was surprised at night by the enemy under Colonel Norton of Southwick. He surrendered without a shot.

In the eighteenth century there was a further disaster when hot embers from a fire fell into the powder room and the resulting explosion killed seventeen people. In 1850 the advent of Napoleon III occasioned the improvement of the defences of Portsmouth, and Southsea was given two outer ramparts.

The building was garrisoned in both world wars, was bought

by Portsmouth Corporation in 1960 and was opened to the public in 1967. Inside there are maps, armour and local history displays. Nearby are the Overlord Embroidery and the D-Day Museum.

Portsmouth City Council. Open throughout the year.

Titchfield

The foundation stone of the abbey was laid in 1219 and its church consecrated in 1238. At the Dissolution of the Monasteries (1537-8) the abbey was surrendered to the Crown and was given to Thomas Wriothesley, Earl of Southampton, by Henry VIII. He converted the abbey into a fortified mansion, 'Palace House' (later Place House), incorporating the nave of the original church. In 1741 the house was sold to the Deline family, who used much of the stone to build elsewhere. The building has been in a state of disrepair since 1810.

English Heritage. Open throughout the year.

Winchester

The ancient capital of England had, to the north-west of the cathedral, a castle which was burnt down in 1141. A new one was built and was the scene of Queen Matilda's rescue by the Earl of Gloucester and sixty men during her war with King Stephen. Today the Great Hall is the courthouse and is open to the public. It contains 'King Arthur's Round Table', which may well have been constructed in the sixteenth century.

Open throughout the year.

HEREFORD AND WORCESTER

Croft

Approached by a long oak avenue, Croft Castle is mostly a fourteenth and fifteenth-century building with four large round towers. It was Gothicised in the mid eighteenth century when it passed from the Croft family to Richard Knight, son of a Shropshire mine owner.

The Crofts were warriors, Sir Richard Croft, whose tomb can be seen in the church, was a veteran of Tewkesbury, Stoke and Mortimer's Cross, the last named battle being fought a few miles to the south-west of the castle. One of his descendants was comptroller of Queen Elizabeth I's household and one of a later generation was killed at Stokesay fighting for Charles I. The Crofts were forced to sell the castle in 1746 but bought it back in 1923.

National Trust. Open April to October.

Goodrich

Near the Gloucestershire border, Goodrich is the most imposing ruin in the county, standing on a spur overlooking the

Wye. The keep of the mid twelfth century is the oldest surviving part; most of the castle was reconstructed of red sandstone in the thirteenth century. Entered by a barbican which is at an angle to the main gateway, it must have been a formidable castle to storm as the two drawbridges swing on central pivots dipping down into pits between the barbican and the main gatehouse. There is a great hall 65 feet (20 m) long and a chapel with a room above overlooking the gatehouse.

The Earl of Pembroke, a supporter of King John and governor to Henry III, acquired Goodrich in 1204. His sons left no male issue and after their deaths his eldest daughter succeeded to the estate with her husband Warren de Mont Cenis. Their son William supported Simon de Montfort and forfeited his estates after being captured by Henry III at Kenilworth. Henry granted the property to William de Valence and later it passed to the Talbots, who lived here until the sixteenth century. During the Civil War it was garrisoned briefly by Parliamentary troops, but was then held for Charles I by Sir Henry Lingen until 1646, when it was captured by increased Parliamentary opposition and slighted by artillery.

English Heritage. Open throughout the year.

Longtown

One of the best preserved of the ruins in the county, Longtown keep stands on a high mound, once the site of a Roman fort, off the A465 near Abergavenny. The keep, mostly thirteenth- and fourteenth-century, has two storeys and three projecting buttresses, in one of which is a spiral staircase. The entrance was on the first floor with steps outside, now destroyed. There were two baileys, and the keep was on the apex of the inner bailey.

It belonged to the de Lacy family and passed by marriage to John de Verdon, one of Edward I's crusaders. When he died it passed to his granddaughter Elizabeth and her husband, Bartholomew de Burghersh, who was knighted for his service in the French wars of Edward III. Their son Thomas supported Richard II and lost both his land and his life for his loyalty. Longtown then passed to the Nevilles, in whose hands it remained for many centuries.

Unrestricted access.

Pembridge

A few miles to the north of Monmouth at Welsh Newton is the thirteenth-century moated castle of Ralph de Pembridge. During the reign of Edward III Richard Pembridge, Lord Warden of the Cinque Ports, lived here. He fought at Poitiers

and Crecy and was buried in Hereford Cathedral. Occupied by both sides during the Civil War, the castle was slighted but was repaired in 1675 by George Kemble.
Open May to September, Thursdays only.

Richard's Castle

Built by Richard Fitzscrub before the Norman conquest, Richard's Castle stands on the Herefordshire bank of the Teme overlooking Ludlow. It is a massive earthwork with a wall across the top and a semicircular wall round the perimeter. Most of the stone has long since vanished but one piece still stands 12 feet (3.7 m) high and there are signs of the wall that enclosed the church.

HERTFORDSHIRE

Berkhamsted

Near the railway station, Berkhamsted is one of the most important castles in England, although little remains today except the motte and bailey and a rare double moat. William the Conqueror gave the Saxon castle at Berkhamsted to his brother Robert, Count of Mortain, who built a strong keep on top of a motte. It had its own well and staircase. The 2 acre (0.8 ha) bailey was enclosed in the twelfth and thirteenth centuries by a massive wall interspersed with half-circular defensive towers. The entrance was at the south (not the present entrance but across a causeway) and there was a small gate over two drawbridges to the north-east. The most unusual features of Berkhamsted are the earth platforms outside the north moat. These are believed to be mangonel platforms built by the French army that attacked and captured the castle in 1216. They may have been part of the defences but, if so, why were they outside and not inside the moat?

The Earl of Cornwall lived here after the Count of Mortain's death, as did Thomas à Becket when he was Lord Chancellor. King John obtained the castle from the property of Richard I's wife, Berengaria, and spent about £250 on repairs. His queen was here when the barons and the Dauphin's French army attacked and captured the castle. John's second son, Richard, Earl of Cornwall, inherited it and built a three-storey tower and numerous apartments for his family. King Edward I granted it to his queen, and in 1309 Edward II gave it to Piers Gaveston.

During the building of Windsor Castle, Berkhamsted was an important royal palace. The Black Prince spent his last days here in 1376 and the captive King John of France was brought here from Somerton. The final inhabitant of note was Cicely, Duchess of York, who made it her home until she died in 1496. Queen Elizabeth I leased it to Sir Edward Carey for the rent of a red rose each year in memory of Cicely, the 'Rose of Raby', who was born a Lancastrian but married a Yorkist. Carey built nearby Berkhamsted Place out of stones from the castle, which remained part of the Duchy of Cornwall until 1930, when it passed to the Commissioners of Works.

English Heritage. Open throughout the year.

Hertford

Hertford Castle was built by William the Conqueror soon after 1066 to guard the ford where the Great North Road crossed the river Lea about 20 miles (32 km) north of London. The internal buildings of the castle were demolished early in the seventeenth century: all that remains is the gatehouse, built in 1463 and which is now the council offices, the Norman motte, the postern gate and most of the curtain walls, over 20 feet (6 m) high.

During the Barons' War against King John, Hertford was besieged by the Dauphin Louis, who captured it from the king's forces. In 1304 the Castle and Honour of Hertford were granted to Queen Margaret and it was used as a royal palace until the accession of James I in 1603. During this period it was used by the kings and queens of England. It was also used as a royal prison for David II of Scotland (after his defeat at Neville's Cross in 1346), for John of France (after the battle of Poitiers in 1356), and for Margaret of Anjou, the queen of Henry VI (after the Yorkist victory at St Albans in 1455). In 1360 the castle was granted to John of Gaunt and was part of the Duchy of Lancaster until 1628.

Queen Elizabeth I held the Law Courts here when there was plague in London. During the reign of Charles I it passed to William, Earl of Salisbury, but it was leased to various occupants, particularly the East India College in the reign of George III. Today the gatehouse with its four towers stands in a pleasant park. The windows and the south-west wing were added in the late eighteenth century and the west wing was built in 1936, all this work being in the Gothic style to match the original gatehouse.

Grounds open daily. Gatehouse open occasionally between May and September.

ISLE OF WIGHT

Carisbrooke

William the Conqueror gave the lordship of the Isle of Wight to William Fitzosbern, who built his castle on the site of a Saxon burgh. The land was granted to Richard de Redvers in 1100, by which time a motte and bailey castle, eventually to have a stone shell-keep and curtain wall around the bailey, was under construction. His son Earl Baldwin retreated here after his defeat at Exeter in 1136 when he was fighting for the Empress Matilda, Henry I's daughter, against Stephen. The castle was besieged by Stephen and surrendered when the water supply gave out. In 1377 the French invaders burnt Yarmouth, Newport and Newtown but failed to take Carisbrooke. The French commander was killed by a crossbow bolt shot from the west wall and they withdrew in return for a payment of a thousand marks to the troops. During the Wars of the Roses Carisbrooke belonged to the Duke of Gloucester, the Duke of Somerset and Lord Scales, all of whom were convicted of high treason. During Elizabeth I's reign elaborate surveying and strengthening were carried out against the threat of possible Spanish invasion.

The most famous person to stay at Carisbrooke was Charles I. He fled here in November 1647 but after plotting with the Scots he found himself a prisoner. Two attempts to escape, planned by his page, Henry Firebrace, failed, the first when he got stuck in the window of his bedroom, the Constable's Chambers. The second attempt (to loosen the bar of his window and bribe the guards) was betrayed by two of the guards. Finally, after a year on the island, the king was moved to Hurst Castle in Hampshire, from where he left for Whitehall and his execution in January 1649. Two of Charles's young children, Princess Elizabeth and Prince Henry, were imprisoned here after his death. Elizabeth died in September 1650 of an illness and young Henry was allowed to join his brother Charles in Holland in 1652.

Princess Beatrice, youngest daughter of Queen Victoria, was the last governor of the Isle of Wight to live at Carisbrooke. Her living accommodation included the great hall and the rooms above it, which now house an Isle of Wight museum. The well house contains a donkey-powered treadwheel which dates from Elizabethan times.

English Heritage. Open throughout the year.

Yarmouth

Behind the George Hotel, Yarmouth Castle was built in 1547 by Henry VIII and was one of the chain of forts erected to defend the south coast against French attack after the alliance of France and the Holy Roman Empire in 1538. It is different from Cowes and Hurst castles because it is square, and it differs from earlier castles in being built with cannon in mind. It has the first arrowhead bastion in England and an earth bank in the north

hall for supporting heavy guns at second-floor level. The living quarters were built in 1632.
English Heritage. Open throughout the year.

KENT

Allington

Just before Maidstone, after the turning off the motorway from London, a lane leads down through a new housing estate to one of the most beautiful castles in southern England. It is now a Carmelite friary. In 1282 Stephen of Penchester obtained a licence to crenellate 'with a wall of stone and lime and hold thus strengthened their house at Alinton'. A copy of the sealed document hangs on the chapel wall today. Penchester built the great hall and Solomon's Tower opposite.

The Wyatts were the best known inhabitants of Allington. Sir Henry Wyatt, a friend of Henry VII and Henry VIII, bought the castle in 1492, adding the Tudor building and the long gallery. His son Thomas was a poet and friend of Anne Boleyn. His son, also called Thomas, led the rebellion against Queen Mary's intended Spanish marriage. His father-in-law, Lord Cobham, was forced to join Wyatt when the rebels stormed his castle at Cooling. The rebellion ended with a march on London. Wyatt and his men were separated and many deserted; Wyatt was executed together with the other leaders of the revolt.

Allington now passed to the Crown and the great hall, chapel and north-east tower were burnt down. For a time John Astley, Master of the Jewels to Elizabeth I, lived here but the Astleys eventually sold it to the Marshams and in 1905 it was bought by Lord Conway, who spent twenty-five years restoring it to its present condition.
Order of Carmelites. Open throughout the year.

Canterbury

Canterbury was the first important town to submit to William the Conqueror after Hastings in 1066, and a motte and bailey castle was then constructed. The motte survives as the mound known as Dane John (i.e. donjon) in the gardens close to the city wall, not far from the subsequent Canterbury Castle, which can be found at the end of Castle Street. The early stone keep here dates from about 1100. In medieval times the Roman Worth Gate gave access to the castle grounds but was blocked in 1548 and demolished in 1791. The castle fell into disuse in 1600. The well preserved city walls date from the Roman period but were extensively repaired in the fourteenth century.
Canterbury City Council. Castle grounds open daily.

Chilham

On A252 between Canterbury and Charing, the keep of Chilham Castle stands next to the Jacobean house of the same name.

Viscount Massereene and Ferrard. The keep and house are not open. Gardens open to the public Easter to October. Falconry displays.

Deal

The Reformation, the dissolution of the monasteries and the alliance between France and the Holy Roman Empire made Henry VIII's England liable to attack from abroad. To counter this, the south coast was fortified by a series of circular forts, each designed to hold a captain and twenty-four men. Deal is larger than Walmer and Sandown and has three tiers. A dry moat surrounds six semicircular bastions and inside this are six smaller bastions with a top storey from which further guns could be fired. The central stair provided a means of escape as it connects by passages with the outer bastion and there is a sally-port leading into the moat. There was also an oven for heating cannonballs, a devastating means of attacking wooden ships.

The only time the castle saw any fighting was in 1648, during the Second Civil War, when Sandown, Deal and Walmer castles were fortified for the king and part of the fleet supplied them with men, munitions and food. Colonel Rich attacked Walmer with an army of two thousand but as he had no artillery the Royalists held out for some time before surrendering. Deal held out for a few more weeks and in August a strong naval force attempted to relieve the garrison. The Royalist commander, Major-General Gibson, was captured with one hundred men, so the following day the garrison surrendered. Sandown Castle capitulated shortly after.

During the eighteenth century the present battlements were added for aesthetic reasons and a governor's lodge was constructed on the seaward side. This was rebuilt in 1802 for Lord Carrington but in 1941 a bomb demolished it and the castle was later restored to its original form. An archaeological museum occupies the gatehouse.

English Heritage. Open throughout the year.

Dover

Continuously fortified from the early iron age and Roman times until 1958, Dover Castle is one of the strongest in England and, because of its position, is second only to the Tower of London in military importance. The Roman lighthouse, or Pharos, still stands next to the church of St. Mary-in-Castro. The

Saxon fortress had a gatehouse, enceinte and well.

The Normans built twenty-seven towers in the outer wall and fourteen square watchtowers in the inner wall. The cliffs form the seaward wall, so there was no moat, although the entrance bridge straddles a dry ditch. The first constable of Dover, appointed by William I, was John de Fiennes. He was assisted by eight knights, who were granted land elsewhere on the condition that they provided a garrison on a rota basis throughout the year.

King Stephen died in Dover in 1154 and Henry II constructed the inner bailey wall and the vast keep, which now houses a model of the battlefield of Waterloo and a collection of arms. Hubert de Burgh defended Dover for King John against Louis, Dauphin of France, in 1216. The French attacked the northern gate, which they breached with a mine, and would have entered had not de Burgh blocked it with timber. In 1265, during the de Montfort rebellion, Dover was in rebel hands but twelve prisoners from Lewes managed to capture two of the towers and helped Prince Edward (later Edward I) to retake the castle.

During the Civil War a Royalist garrison surrendered to a party of twelve Parliamentarians led by a local merchant called Drake. They climbed over the north-east wall and talked the Royalist commander into surrender. Another 120 men were rushed in from Canterbury and by the time the Royalists had rallied Drake had the castle secured.

In 1794 the circular Valence and Mortimer towers were added, and another tower, which still remains though in a much altered state, was built over Colton's Gate, which leads to the Pharos.

During the Napoleonic Wars Lieutenant Burgoyne, Inspector General of Fortifications, installed gun positions on the keep roof, built many bastions and excavated a series of underground passages defended by an ingenious system of remote-controlled doors which could trap attackers. Provision was made for a total of 231 guns of all sizes to defend the castle. The constables of the castle in the nineteenth century included William Pitt, the Duke of Wellington and Lord Palmerston. The castle was an important military headquarters in the Second World War.

English Heritage. Open throughout the year.

Eynsford

In the Darent valley on A225, Eynsford Castle stands opposite the Castle Inn. It was built by William d'Eynsford and is D-shaped with flint walls 30 feet (9 m) high in places. D'Eynsford quarrelled with Thomas à Becket but after the archbishop's murder he was filled with remorse and vowed never to live in his castle again. The keep was excavated and was

discovered to have originally been a timber tower built over a well, replaced at a later date by a stone shell-keep.
English Heritage. Open throughout the year.

Hever

Near Edenbridge, Hever is one of the finest inhabited castles in England. A licence to crenellate was granted to Sir John de Cobham in 1384. In 1462 the castle was bought by Sir Geoffrey Bullen (Boleyn), Lord Mayor of London, who made considerable alterations to it. The building was completed by his grandson, Sir Thomas Boleyn, father of Henry VIII's unfortunate queen, Anne. Henry first met her in the garden at Hever. They were married in 1533 and in 1536 she was arrested, accused of adultery and executed. Henry then married Jane Seymour, who produced the son and heir the king wished for so dearly.

After Sir Thomas Boleyn's death, the castle passed to Anne of Cleves, Henry's fourth wife, and when she died it was sold to Sir Edward Waldegrave. From the Waldegraves it passed to Sir William Humfreys, Lord Mayor of London in 1714, and then to Sir Timothy Waldo. The castle today owes its appearance and beautiful gardens to the first Viscount Astor, who bought it in 1903 and built a mock Tudor village for his guests in the grounds. The contents include Anne Boleyn's sad last letter to Henry, a room of torture instruments and some fine paintings.
Broadland Properties Ltd. Open regularly March to November.

Leeds

Just outside Maidstone, on the main road to Canterbury, the magnificent castle at Leeds is surrounded by an artificial lake. It was built by the Saxons and after the Norman conquest was enlarged by the de Crèvecoeur family. During the Barons' War of Simon de Montfort, Robert de Crèvecoeur changed sides and was dispossessed by Henry III, who granted the castle to Roger de Leyburn.

Later Edward I owned Leeds and his son Edward II gave it to one of his barons, Lord Badlesmere, with his queen Isabella nominally in possession. However the constable, Walter Culpeper, refused permission for the queen and her party to enter and six of the queen's men were killed trying to do so. The king laid siege to Leeds and Badlesmere, attempting to relieve it, was forced to withdraw. Culpeper was captured and executed, along with eleven of his men.

Reverting to the Crown, Leeds was used as a prison for the unfortunate Richard II for a short time, and later for the wife of Henry IV. Henry VI was here in 1431 when his aunt Eleanor of Gloucester was tried for 'necromancy, witchcraft, heresy and treason' in front of Archbishop Chichele. She was sentenced to life imprisonment in the castle. During the seventeenth century there were Dutch and French prisoners here under the charge of John Evelyn, who 'flooded the dry moat, made a new drawbridge and brought spring water into the court'. It later belonged to the Culpepers, one of whom was Governor of Virginia from 1680 to 1683.

In 1926 Leeds was acquired by the Hon. Lady Baillie, who brought in Stèfan Boudin, a French designer, to help decorate the castle. Leeds has a gloriette, connected by a double bridge passage to the main castle, itself on an island and linked by bridge to the inner and outer barbicans. In the Second World War the castle was a hospital and convalescent home.

Leeds Castle Foundation. Open regularly March to October.

Lympne

The present castle incorporates the Square Tower, which is very old and believed to be the watchtower of the Roman fort of the Saxon Shore 300 feet (90 m) below (known in Roman times as *Portus Lemanis*). The Great Hall, built in 1360, replaced an early Norman one of the late eleventh century and the Great Tower was built between 1360 and 1420. Minor restoration was undertaken in 1905 by Sir Robert Lorrimer, who also built the New Wing. Most of the castle lies untouched since the fourteenth century.

Harry Margary. Open regularly May to September and Bank holidays.

Reculver

A small fort was built at Reculver, near Herne Bay, by the Romans in the first century. In the third century it was enlarged as a fort of the Saxon Shore. Originally known as *Regulbium*, it is famous today for the remains of its church, founded by Egbert in 669. The south and east walls remain in parts but the north wall vanished under the sea many years ago. A copy of a charter granting the monastery of Egbert at Reculver to Christ Church, Canterbury, and signed by Dunstan, Abbot of Glastonbury, can be seen today in Canterbury Cathedral library. The twin towers of the church, which was demolished in 1809, were kept as a landmark. According to legend they were erected by an abbess whose sister was shipwrecked off the Reculver cliffs.

English Heritage. Church open normal hours.

Richborough

Just outside Sandwich, one mile from the Canterbury road, the massive Roman walls of Richborough look down over the railway line and the site of the old Roman port of *Rutupiae*. Here

Claudius landed with his invasion army in AD 43 and built a supply base. A house and three surrounding ditches were built in the second half of the third century. The walls date from about 287, when Richborough was one of the castles erected by the Count of the Saxon Shore. St Augustine is supposed to have landed at Ebbsfleet, 3 miles (5 km) from Richborough, in 597 to meet Ethelbert of Kent. The imprint of his foot was kept on a stone and a chapel was built by the Saxons to house the relic. Excavations during the 1920s revealed a number of coins and skeletons, including the grave of a Roman soldier with shield, spear and sword. The principal finds are in the museum on the site and include a remarkable Anglo-Saxon sword with a blade made of strips of iron welded together.

English Heritage. Open throughout the year.

Rochester

On a bend in the river Medway, Rochester was once a Roman camp commanding a bridge on the road from London to Dover. Later it became a Saxon castle, *Hrofe Caestre*, which consisted of a fortified enclosure of 7 acres (2.8 ha) and a motte known as Boley Hill. The manor was bestowed on Odo, Bishop of Bayeux, by William I but the first castle was built in about 1080 by Bishop Gundulf.

Rochester keep was constructed about 1126 by William de Corbeuil in an enceinte measuring 160 by 130 yards (146 by 119 m). It is over 100 feet (30 m) high and has a square forebuilding and walls 12 feet (3.7 m) thick. This was the first great square keep to be constructed in an English castle and it was soon put to the test. William d'Albini held it against King John for three months in 1215 and only by undermining the south-west tower did the king's forces get into the bailey and dislodge the garrison from the keep.

In 1216 the French Dauphin Louis recaptured Rochester for the barons, but the castle successfully withstood a siege by Simon de Montfort in 1264. In 1381 it was captured by Wat Tyler's rebels, who were supported by the local townsfolk. After this it fell into decay although Edward IV tried to repair it.

In 1883 it was bought by the Corporation of Rochester and opened to the public.

English Heritage. Open throughout the year.

Saltwood

On top of the hill above Hythe, Saltwood Castle is tucked away from view on the other side of the road from the church. It is recorded that Aesc, son of Hengist, 'built a castle in this place' in 488, but during the Roman occupation it was important, as it stood just off Stane Street. Saltwood was then a fortified port,

Hythe being under water.

The present castle was built by Henry de Essex, Henry II's standard-bearer.

Later owners included Archbishop Courtenay. He built the twin-towered gatehouse, which was converted in Victorian times by the Deedes family and is now the inhabited part of the building. Cranmer, the last archbishop to live here, gave it to Henry VIII in 1540. Forty years later an earthquake rendered it uninhabitable, until restored by the Deedeses and by Lady Conway, who reroofed the Archbishop's Hall.

Hon. Alan Clark. Closed to the public.

Scotney

Originally a fourteenth-century moated castle built by Roger Ashburnham in the reign of Richard II, Scotney, near Lamberhurst, is a romantic round tower set in the garden of a late Georgian mansion. In 1422 it was acquired by Archbishop Chichele who gave it to his niece and her husband, Thomas Darell of Ashford. The Darells were Catholics and secret chambers were built to hide their priests. One of these, Father Blount, with Bray his servant, remained hidden for a week while the Darells were out of the castle and it was occupied by their enemies. Today it is famous for its gardens.

National Trust. Open regularly, March to November.

Sissinghurst

Not far from Cranbrook, Sissinghurst was built by the Speaker of the House of Commons, Sir John Baker, in about 1530. During the Seven Years War it held French prisoners of war and today only the Tudor gatehouse and moat remain in the famous garden restored by the late Miss V. Sackville-West.

National Trust. Open April to October, except Mondays.

Sutton Valence

Protecting the road from Rochester to Rye, Sutton Valence is a few miles south of Maidstone on A274. The ruined castle stands on a hill by the church. Only a portion of the keep remains.

The castle was built by one of Henry III's many unpopular half-brothers, William de Valence, who married a Pembroke heiress and later became Earl of Pembroke. During de Montfort's rebellion, William supported Henry III at Lewes and after the battle of Evesham was made governor of Goodrich Castle (Hereford and Worcester). Three Pembrokes owned Sutton Valence until it passed to the Cliffords. When Mildred Clifford, who had four husbands, died, her first husband, Sir Edward Harper, inherited it. He sold it to Sir Edward Hales, whose family lived here for many years. In 1956 the site was excavated and pottery dating from 1150 was discovered, together with parts of the forebuilding and staircase.

Tonbridge

Richard Fitzgilbert built a castle on a prehistoric mound at Tonbridge. It was surrounded by a moat fed from the river. During 1088 the castle held out against William Rufus, but Fitzgilbert was wounded during the siege and the castle surrendered. He died in Normandy in 1091. In the thirteenth century Richard de Clare built the gatehouse which stands today.

Held for Parliament during the Civil War, the castle was not demolished until 1793, when it was bought by Thomas Hooker of Peckham. He constructed the present Gothic building, now used as municipal offices, next to the gatehouse. The bailey is a garden and only a small piece of the wall remains.
Open regularly, May to mid September.

Upnor

In 1561 an Elizabethan fort was constructed on the river Medway at Upnor, near Rochester. It was a long three-storey building with a tower at each end and a ravelin in front with gun platforms and stockade. The only time the guns fired against an enemy was in 1667 when de Ryter invaded the Medway. His leading ships crossed over the chain at Upnor and set fire to two guard ships, the *Mathias* and the *Charles V.* Two other ships, the *Royal Charles* and the frigate *Unity,* were captured and four more were set on fire almost under the noses of Upnor Castle's inefficient gunners. This, according to Evelyn, was 'as dreadful a spectacle as Englishmen ever saw and a dishonour never to be wiped off'.
English Heritage. Open throughout the year.

Walmer

On the edge of the beach where Julius Caesar landed in 55 BC, Walmer Castle was built for Henry VIII by the engineer Stephan von Haschenperg under the oversight of Sir Edward Ryngley, to guard the coast against invasion. Not as large as Deal or the three other 'castles of the Downs', Walmer consists of four large bastions with a central circular one.

Since the eighteenth century Walmer has been the official residence of the Lord Warden of the Cinque Ports and three

Lords Warden, the Duke of Dorset, Earl Granville and William Pitt, made considerable alterations. In Pitt's time Lady Stanhope planned the garden and Granville added the tower by the entrance and thirteen extra rooms.

The most famous occupant of the castle was the Duke of Wellington, who lived here, apart from his wife, in his final years and died in a chair in his room upstairs on 14th September 1852. He was not a believer in comfort and his bed is remarkably small for he believed that 'when it is time to turn round it is time to turn out'. In the upstairs dome landing are pictures of all the Lords Warden, who include W. H. Smith and Winston Churchill. The collection of objects associated with Wellington is unrivalled and includes the T. H. Lucas Collection.

English Heritage. Open throughout the year. Closed when Lord Warden is in residence.

West Malling

Near where the A20 crosses the A228 between Rochester and Tonbridge, St Leonard's Tower is the only surviving part of the castle of Gundulf, Bishop of Rochester. (Gundulf was responsible for building the White Tower in the Tower of London as well as the abbey at East Malling.) The structure dates from about 1080 and is 60 feet (18 m) high with four Norman-arched windows side by side on the first floor and a larger window above; the top storey is in ruins.

Once used as a jail, the tower later became a hop store. In the seventeenth century it belonged to the Rainey family, who sold it to the Honywoods.

Open to the public at all times. Key at Number 1 Park Cottages. Admission free.

LANCASHIRE

Clitheroe

A small Norman keep and part of a wall still remain of Roger de Poitou's castle in the Ribble valley, first mentioned in 1102. He was the son of Roger de Montgomery, who commanded the centre divisions of William's army at Hastings. Later it passed to the de Lacys and Alice, last of this family, married a Plantagenet; he was beheaded in 1322 by Edward II, after which the castle became part of the Duchy of Lancaster. Clitheroe Castle Museum adjoins the castle.

Hoghton Tower

An Elizabethan mansion with two courtyards was probably built on the site of an earlier castle here. It was fortified during the Civil War and the gatehouse was used as a powder room; two hundred men were killed when this blew up and for many years the house was a ruin.

Sir Bernard de Hoghton, Bt. Open regularly Easter to October.

Lancaster

Originally a Roman fort, probably built by Hadrian, Lancaster then became a Saxon stronghold. The stone castle was built by the Norman Roger de Poitou, who owned a large area of Lancashire at that time. In 1102 he forfeited his land for supporting the barons' rebellion against Henry I and the castle passed to the Crown. King John held court here in 1206 and was responsible for much of the building. In the fourteenth century it belonged to John of Gaunt, but he does not appear to have lived here. His son Henry Bolingbroke, after deposing Richard II and becoming Henry IV, established the Duchy of Lancaster. The land bestowed on the Duchy was deemed a separate inheritance from the Crown and the castle has been part of the Duchy ever since.

From the mid seventeenth century the castle has been a prison and criminal court. During the Civil War it remained in Parliamentary hands although besieged by the Royalists in 1648 under Sir Thomas Tyldesley; it held out and was partially demolished by order the following year. In 1715 it was occupied briefly by Jacobites, who set the prisoners free. In 1798 the Crown Court was built and in the dock is the branding iron. Prisoners sentenced to be branded had their left hand put in the clamp and a large M pressed on the fleshy part of their hand below the thumb. It was last used in 1801.

The keep is the oldest part of the castle and the upper part was restored in 1585. The first floor contains the old Shire Hall and the ground floor the prison chapel.

The dungeons are on view (five of them were discovered as late as 1931) and the gatehouse, dating from 1400, has the coat of arms of Prince Hal, later Henry V, and, in the niche a statue of John of Gaunt, put there in 1822.

Open every weekday except when courts are sitting. Prison area not shown.

Lathom House

3 miles (5 km) from Ormskirk, only the stable block of the eighteenth-century house and the slightly restored chapel of 1500 survive. The original house was built on a low, boggy site and surrounded with a wide moat and a thick wall. It had nine

towers and the Earl of Derby armed each with six cannon. Palisades were erected between the moat and the wall, and the gatehouse had two flanking towers. The house itself — large enough to 'receive three kings' — had a high tower known as the Eagle Tower. In 1642 the Earl was in the Isle of Man but his wife and children were at Lathom with a strong garrison. Rigby, the local Parliamentary leader, tried to persuade her to surrender and when she refused he turned a large mortar on the house, but the garrison captured this during the night and took it inside. Finally the Earl with Prince Rupert relieved Lathom in May 1844 and the Countess and her children went to Man. Lathom held out after Marston Moor until the treachery of an Irish soldier led to its surrender. It was completely destroyed and some of the timbers were used for a scaffold for the execution of Lord Derby after his capture in the retreat from Worcester in 1651.

Lathom chapel is open at all times.

LEICESTERSHIRE

Ashby-de-la-Zouch

One of the most famous of England's castles, Ashby-de-la-Zouch was the scene of Sir Walter Scott's famous jousting tournament in *Ivanhoe*.

The castle did not begin to take shape until the twelfth century, when the Zouch family from Brittany built a stone hall and solar. The Mortimers from Shropshire inherited the manor in 1314.

During the Wars of the Roses Ashby belonged to the Earl of Ormond until he was beheaded by the Yorkists after the battle of Towton. His forfeited estates were given to Lord Hastings, a favourite of Edward IV, who lived at nearby Kirby Muxloe. Hastings set about building a large tower at Ashby and also obtained licences to crenellate Kirby and another house he owned at Bagworth. Not wanting to demolish any of the existing buildings, Lord Hastings built a chapel on the end of the solar and connected it to a priest's room. Both these buildings formed, with the new tower, a south courtyard.

In 1483 Lord Hastings was accused of treason by Richard III and was beheaded. His son escaped to fight for Henry Tudor at Bosworth and Ashby remained in the Hastings family. In 1569 Mary, Queen of Scots, was brought to Ashby after the Northern Rising and in 1617 her son, James I, was entertained here by George Hastings, Earl of Huntingdon, who spent so much on the king's seventeen-day visit that he had to sell twenty-four manors and thirty-two lordships to pay for it.

During the Civil War Ashby was garrisoned by Colonel Hastings, Lord Loughborough, for Charles I. He built Mount

House in Leicester Road for his horsemen and connected it to the castle by an underground passage. Another passage, still existing, ran from the Hastings Tower to the kitchen block. In 1644 Lord Grey's Parliamentary forces captured the town but Lord Loughborough held out for Charles. After Naseby in June 1645 the Royalist cavalry arrived with the king, but, although hard pressed at the time, it was not until 28th February 1646 that the garrison surrendered. Two years later Parliament ordered the castle to be blown up with gunpowder. The south wall was destroyed and all the outer part of the rest of the building, so that it is difficult to appreciate the great strength of the castle today.

It has been called 'the maiden garrison' for it was never captured, only surrendered on terms.

English Heritage. Entrance in Upper Church Street, Ashby-de-la-Zouch. Open throughout the year.

Kirby Muxloe

Lord Hastings, favourite of Edward IV, obtained a licence to fortify an old manor house at Kirby in 1474. He had obtained the property from the Earl of Ormond, a Lancastrian who was killed after the battle at Towton. The old manor's great hall was retained and a fortified wall with a square corner turret and a gatehouse was constructed. The west tower has three storeys with unusual early gunports.

The accounts for building Kirby Muxloe still survive, and a total of £1,088 17s 6¾d was spent in four years, continuing after 1483, when Hastings was executed for treason. The brickwork is very fine and was probably done by Flemings under Roger Bowlett and their master mason Couper, who worked at Tattershall. The Hastings coat of arms shows a maunch or sleeve and the bricklayers worked this into the pattern of the gatehouse's north-west octagon turret. In 1913 the castle was presented to the Commissioners of Works.

English Heritage. Open throughout the year.

Oakham

The Great Hall of Oakham Castle is one of the finest examples of Norman domestic architecture in England. It is all that survives of an important early medieval manor house and was built by Walkelin de Ferrers soon after 1180. Traces of an earlier motte and bailey castle can also be seen, and the present bailey is enclosed by a bank and wall. Within this there were once many other buildings, but they were probably mostly in ruins by about 1500.

The Ferrers family held Oakham until 1252. It passed through many hands, reverting to the crown several times, until in 1596 it was sold for the first time. In 1621 it was bought by George Villiers, later Duke of Buckingham, and in 1687 by Daniel Finch, Earl of Nottingham. It remained in the Finch family until 1939, later coming into public ownership.

The walls of the castle are hung with over two hundred presentation horseshoes, paid as forfeits to the lord of the manor by peers of the realm passing through the lordship for the first time. The origins of the custom, which is still valid today, are unknown, but the earliest documented horseshoe was given by Edward IV, probably in about 1470.

Leicestershire Museums, Art Galleries and Records Service. Open daily except Mondays.

LINCOLNSHIRE

Lincoln

Lincoln Castle was built in 1068 on a Roman site; 166 houses had to be demolished to make room for it. Henry II was crowned here in 1155. The east and west gates and wall and Norman shell-keep are still standing.

Open throughout the year.

Old Bolingbroke

Near Horncastle, Old Bolingbroke is a tiny village below a small hill with a few stones near the church marking the site of the castle of the de Gaunts, Dukes of Lancaster.

The castle was described by Gervase Holles in the seventeenth century. 'The building lies within a square area (the outer bailey) within the walls containing about an acre and a half (0.6 ha) (outer bailey surrounded by a moat); the building is very uniform. It hath four strong forts or ramparts wherein are many rooms and lodgings; the passage from one to another lying upon the walls which are embattled about. There be likewise two watchtowers all covered in lead. The entrance to it is very stately over a fair drawbridge; the gatehouse a very uniform and strong building.' Holles remarks on the three dungeons or prisons and a ghost — 'a certain spirit in the likeness of a hare'.

During the Civil War the Royalist garrison was isolated, as most of the eastern counties supported Parliament. In October 1643 the Earl of Manchester ordered the castle to surrender in a rudely worded message. Back came the reply 'Bugbear words must not win a castle nor should make them quit a place'. A few days later Widdrington and Henderson led a Royalist force from Newark to relieve the castle garrison. Manchester, supported by Fairfax and Cromwell with their troopers, met him at Winceby, where the Royalists were defeated.

The castle was abandoned and only the gatehouse remained

for some time. In 1815 this too collapsed so that it is difficult to imagine the present fragments as ever constituting a building fit enough 'to entertain a very great Prince with all his train'. *Ruins open at all reasonable times.*

South Kyme Tower

A few miles from Boston on A17 to Sleaford, South Kyme is a small village with a castle keep tower standing beside a Georgian farmhouse.

Tattershall

Lincolnshire castles tend to have tall towers to serve as lookout posts. Tattershall is no exception and is one of the most remarkable surviving pieces of fifteenth-century brickwork in England.

Situated on the river Bain about 13 miles (21 km) from Sleaford on A153 to Horncastle, the great five-storey tower was built by Ralph, Lord Cromwell, in about 1440. It stands on the site of a thirteenth-century castle built by Robert of Tattershall, a descendant of Eudo, the Norman lord of the manor. Ralph inherited the old castle from his father and, using the fortune he made on the Agincourt campaign and later as Treasurer of the King's Exchequer, he built the tower that stands today and which still rises to 100 feet (30 m), and to 112 feet (34 m) to the top of the octagonal machicolated turrets. The walls are 14 feet (4.3 m) thick in places, but the large windows made it impractical for defence against cannon. For this reason it had a double moat, the inner moat being supplied by a small channel from the outer moat. Four carved stone fireplaces kept the building warm. Outside the great chamber on the second floor is a wood and plaster dovecote. On the third floor the heraldic glass in the windows includes the arms of Robert of Tattershall. Altogether there are forty-eight separate rooms, with garderobes on each floor and accommodation for a hundred people. The cost of Tattershall was recorded by William of Worcester as 'above 4,000 marks'.

After Ralph's death the castle passed to his niece Joan, who married Sir Thomas Neville. For a time Henry VII's mother lived here; then in 1520 Henry VIII gave it to the Duke of Suffolk on his marriage to the king's sister. It belonged to the Earls of Lincoln from 1573 to 1693 and descended to the Fortescue family. In 1911 an American syndicate bought the tower and dismantled the fireplaces preparatory to shipping them to the USA. However, Lord Curzon of Kedleston intervened, acquired the castle and, rescuing the fireplaces from London, restored them to their original positions. He bequeathed the building to the National Trust in 1925.
National Trust. Open throughout the year.

NORFOLK

Baconsthorpe

Situated about 3 miles (5 km) east of Holt, off A148 from King's Lynn to Cromer, Baconsthorpe Hall or Castle, the ancient seat of the Heydon family, is now a ruin. On the same site stood a manor belonging to the Bacons of Baconsthorpe, but early in 1400 the Heydon family acquired the property and William Heydon's son John started to build the castle. He did not obtain a licence to crenellate his house so the date is not exactly known, but it is likely to have been about 1450. The inner gatehouse was the work of John and the outer works were built by his grandson Sir Henry Heydon, who was the steward to Cecily, mother of Edward IV. He married the daughter of the Lord Mayor of London, which helped to increase his fortune. Later Heydons took up sheep farming and Sir Christopher Heydon and his son William had to sell part of the estate to pay off their farming debts. Sir William's son, also Christopher, rebuilt parts of the castle in 1600, narrowing the moat. His two sons were soldiers, the younger one, Sir John Heydon, becoming Lieutenant-General of the Ordinance to Charles I. He was a noted mathematician and fought at Edgehill. After the war he was forced to sell most of the castle for building material. The outer gatehouse became a house and the rest of the castle a walled garden.

The original building with its curtain wall had a single moat round its two courts and a lake on the east side. The southern gatehouse, added in the late sixteenth century, had no moat round it. One of its two turrets is still standing, built of flint with ashlar cornering and an unusual ogee-shaped cupola. The inner gatehouse has three storeys and is partly of brick. To the south and west the curtain wall remains with a square corner tower containing a keyhole gunport. The overmantel from the great hall fireplace with its Heydon coat of arms is now in the churchyard and in the church is a large monument to Sir William Heydon, who died in 1592.

English Heritage. Open throughout the year.

Buckenham

At Old Buckenham are earthworks of the old castle used by the Augustine canons in 1146. It has a shell-keep surrounded by a massive earth wall and moat and is worthy of archaeological exploration.

Open at all times. Key to gate from local garage.

Burgh Castle

The Roman fort at the confluence of the rivers Waveney and

Bure has three impressive walls of flint and brick. The Normans built a motte and bailey castle in one corner of the 5 acre (2 ha) court. One of the best Roman remains in Britain, Burgh was known as *Gariannonum*. Later it became a Saxon Shore fort.

Caister

4 miles (6 km) north of Yarmouth off A1064 stand the ruins of Sir John Falstaff's castle built of brick in 1450 out of the ransom money Sir John obtained by capturing a French knight in the Agincourt campaign. The castle passed to John Paston on Sir John's death but the estate was claimed by many others including John Mowbray, Duke of Norfolk. Paston's father, Sir William, was a judge and had been a friend of Sir John's. We know a great deal about the Pastons through the Paston letters, which have survived. One of the family fought for Warwick at the battle of Barnet and went to Calais. Another, his brother, defended Caister, when it was attacked by the Duke of Norfolk in 1469. There were less than thirty defenders against an army of three thousand well armed soldiers. Dame Margaret Paston wrote in haste to her son in London to come with aid: 'Your brother and his fellowship stand in great jeopardy at Caister and lack victuals, Daubeney and Berney be dead, and divers others be greatly hurt, and they fail gunpowder and arrows and the place is sore broken by guns.' Norfolk had to bring in reinforcements from King's Lynn before Caister finally succumbed. For seven years the Pastons gave up the castle and only when Norfolk died suddenly at Framlingham did they return. In 1660 Sir William Paston sold the castle, then ruinous, to the Gurney family.

Caister is designed to withstand a siege. It consists of two rectangular outworks surrounded by a moat that was connected with the river Bure. The entrance was by a west drawbridge to the north outwork and thence by another drawbridge to the main building, part of which remains today. The three-storey tower in the south-west corner rises to 90 feet (27 m). The great hall, lit by six double square-topped windows, butts on to the tower. The north outwork contained the Falstaff college and chantry but only two buttressed walls remain intact today.

Dr P. R. Hill, JP. Open mid May to late September (closed Saturdays). Caister Castle Motor Museum stands in the estate.

Castle Acre

Situated on the old Peddars Way track from Holme-next-the-Sea to Brandon, Castle Acre is primarily noted for its fine priory, founded by William de Warenne in the eleventh century. The castle has a motte and bailey with a horseshoe-shaped moat. The north gate still stands at the top of Bailey Street in the village. It is of Early English style with two towers on each side.

The chapel stood to the east of this gate and until 1800 there was a south gate further down Bailey Street.

When William de Warenne married Gundreda they went on a pilgrimage to Rome. On their return they founded the priory, which was subordinate to the Cistercian monastery at Lewes. Gundreda died in 1085 at the castle and William four years later. In the nineteenth century some workmen building a railway line dug up two coffins which were recognised as those of the de Warennes. The last of this family died in 1347 and the castle has remained a ruin since then.

English Heritage. Open throughout the year.

Castle Rising

4 miles (6 km) north-east of King's Lynn, Castle Rising stands on a mound once washed by the sea.

The Norman keep which remains today was built by William d'Albini, known as William of the Strong Hand because he was said to have pulled out a lion's tongue. He married the widow of Henry I and was created the first Earl of Arundel. His son William inherited the castle and later it passed to the Crown. Queen Isabella came to live here after the death of Mortimer, her lover. From 1358, when she died, until 1397 it belonged to the Black Prince and later to Richard II, ultimately becoming part of the Duchy of Cornwall. Henry VIII granted it to Thomas Howard, Duke of Norfolk, and for many years it remained in the Howard family.

In the reign of Henry III there was trouble in King's Lynn. The Earl of Arundel was entitled to a third part of the customs dues of the port and the garrison of Castle Rising demanded food supplies from the town which were rarely paid for. One year the Earl arrived with an armed band to demand his rights despite the gales that had reduced the wealth of the town that year. The citizens captured him and held him in custody. The rest of the garrison fled back to Castle Rising with the mayor's daughter as a hostage. For many weeks the townsfolk besieged the castle. Their leader was Hal Steele, the Earl's former armourer, and he was able to make mangonels which breached the walls and yielded the castle to the town. The Earl was set free on condition that he no longer claimed his dues and the mayor's daughter was rescued by the armourer.

English Heritage. Open throughout the year.

Norwich

Norwich Castle was built as Crown property in the reign of William the Conqueror and its first constable was probably Ralph Guarder. Guarder led a revolt in 1075 against William the

Conqueror and was defeated by the troops of the bishops of Bayeux and Coutances. Norwich was captured and Ralph Guarder fled to Brittany. A few years later Roger Bigod, the Earl of Norfolk and Suffolk and the new constable of Norwich, held the castle from William II. In 1549 Robert Kett led a rebellion against the Protector Somerset's government; he recruited some four thousand peasants and threatened Norwich. The Earl of Warwick, with the help of German mercenaries, defeated the rebels at Mousehold Heath and Kett was hanged from the castle battlements.

The Norman keep (refaced 1834-9), the entrance tower, the bases of the drum towers of the great gate and three underground rooms of the great gate all remain today, as well as the dry moat and the south bailey. The castle now houses a museum containing archaeology and natural history collections and a fine selection of paintings from the Norwich School.

Norfolk County Council. Open throughout the year.

Weeting

A ruined fortified manor house near Thetford, Weeting Castle dates from the late twelfth century and may have been the home of the Dukes of Brandon.

English Heritage. Open at all reasonable times.

NORTHAMPTONSHIRE

Barnwell

A few miles south of Oundle, Barnwell Castle was originally built by Reginald de Moine in 1132, and the remains consist of a quadrangular court with circular towers at each corner and a large south-eastern gateway flanked by two further towers. It was rebuilt in 1264 by another de Moine and passed to the Montague family. Today it stands in the grounds of the seventeenth century Barnwell Castle, home of HRH the Duke of Gloucester.

Not open to the public.

Rockingham

The most important of the Northamptonshire castles, Rockingham is very close to Corby. It was built by William I, who chose a spur commanding the land between the Nene and the Welland for a shell-keep 100 feet (30 m) wide. The massive twin towers of the gatehouse date from 1275. Rockingham was used as a hunting lodge until the fifteenth century and King John was a frequent visitor. After his death, the constable, the Earl of Albermarle, rebelled against Henry III, but after a siege of over a hundred days Queen Isabella retook it on behalf of her son.

In the sixteenth century Edward Watson constructed the main

house on the old Norman hall. His son, Sir Edward, entertained James I here in 1604. Forty years later Sir Lewis Watson was turned out by Lord Grey of Groby, who fortified the castle for Parliament. At first distrusted by the Royalists, Sir Lewis was tried at Oxford but after a period of imprisonment at Belvoir Castle he won his case and at the Restoration he returned to the castle as Baron Rockingham. He restored the house where his descendants live today, repairing Parliamentarian damage. A tower was added, and other alterations were made by Salvin in the nineteenth century, the Square Tower being built in 1890. *Commander Michael Saunders Watson. Open regularly Easter to September.*

NORTHUMBERLAND

Alnwick

The first Norman owner of Alnwick was probably Gilbert Tyson or de Tesson. He had been William's standard bearer at Hastings, and he was holder of the lands when Malcolm III of Scotland raided the north in 1093. Malcolm was ambushed near Alnwick by Robert Mowbray, the Earl of Northumberland. But in 1095 Mowbray rebelled against William Rufus and was joined by Tyson, who thereby forfeited his lands. Yvo de Vescy received the site in 1096 and began building. His only daughter married Eustace Fitzjohn. Even though Fitzjohn fought on the side of David I and Matilda at the battle of the Standard in 1138, Stephen allowed him to keep Alnwick and by the time of his death in Wales in 1157 the castle was complete.

Eustace de Vescy, who held the castle during the reign of King John, allied himself with the Barons and was one of the twenty-five chosen to see that the terms of Magna Carta were enforced. Alnwick had already been threatened with destruction by the angry king and now was burned when John marched on the north. Before the war was over Eustace was killed by an arrow from a crossbow while besieging Barnard Castle. John de Vescy, grandson of Eustace, continued the feud against the monarchy by supporting Simon de Montfort at Lewes in 1264. But in 1265 at Evesham, when de Montfort was defeated by Prince Edward, John was wounded and captured. Undaunted, he tried to seize back his confiscated estates, was pardoned and joined Prince Edward on crusade before dying in France in 1288. The Scots under Wallace attacked the castle in 1297 and Henry Percy bought it in 1309. In 1402 the Percys captured the Earl of Douglas and other important Scottish prisoners at the battle of Homildon Hill. Angered by Henry IV's demand that he should take charge of the prisoners, Harry Hotspur took advantage of the Glyndwr rebellion in Wales to stage his own revolt but was defeated at Shrewsbury by the future Henry V.

Alnwick avoided destruction during the Civil War because it was never irrevocably committed to either side. In 1755 Hugh, Earl of Northumberland, hired Robert Adam to gothicise the castle and the stone fixtures on the battlements date from this period. Two of the seven round towers forming the keep were pulled down in 1854 and a larger north-west tower, known as the Prudhoe Tower, and the chapel were built to designs by Salvin. *Duke of Northumberland. Open May to September, except Saturdays.*

Aydon

Near Corbridge, Aydon was crenellated by Robert de Raynes of Bolam in 1305. It is a fortified house with an outer bailey and an inner walled bailey. It has been used as a private house and so is in excellent condition.

Bamburgh

The most famous of the castles of the eastern seaboard, Bamburgh appears to be enormous because of its immensely thick walls. In prehistoric times it was a stronghold of the Votadini tribe. It was occupied by the Romans and in 547 became the capital of the Saxon King Ida's kingdom. Ida's grandson Ethelfrith married Bebba and it is assumed that the name Bamburgh is a corruption of Bebbanburgh. Oswald, son of Ethelfrith, united the two kingdoms of Deira and Bernicia after the battle of Heavenfield in 633. It was he who sent to Iona for a missionary and welcomed Aidan to Bamburgh and Holy Island. On 5th August 642 Mercian invaders hung the remains of King Oswald on three wooden stakes and Bamburgh never regained its prominence as capital of the largest British kingdom. The Vikings sacked the fortress in the ninth century. The Normans recognised the military value of the site, and the rock was fortified, probably with a wooden structure. In 1095 the fortress was held by Robert Mowbray against William Rufus. In attempting to escape while under siege, Mowbray was captured and paraded before his wife, who was still in the castle. She surrendered on receiving a message that her husband would lose his eyes if resistance continued. In King Stephen's war the Scots invaded Northumberland and pierced the outer bailey, capturing and killing a hundred defenders. Henry II built the massive keep and strengthened the defences; King John installed a constable, who acquired an evil reputation by robbing passing ships. Henry III built the King's Hall (which was restored completely by Ferguson in about 1900). It has a dais and hammerbeam roof.

The most famous constable was Hotspur, who led out his army to defeat the Scots at Homildon Hill and then plotted with them against the king and lost his life at Shrewsbury in 1403. In the Wars of the Roses Henry VI and his queen, Margaret, escaped to Scotland pursued by the Earl of Warwick. The castle was surrendered to Edward IV but it was immediately retaken and occupied by Queen Margaret. She escaped on hearing of the approach of Warwick's army and left the castle under Sir Ralph Percy's command. In December the siege began and the defenders were soon eating horsemeat. On Christmas Eve they surrendered but broke the treaty and filled the castle with reinforcements. Henry joined the defenders and in June 1464, after the battle of Hexham, Bamburgh became the first English castle to surrender to gunpowder.

Bamburgh was a ruin when it was purchased by Lord Crewe in 1704. Lady Crewe's nephew, Thomas Forster, the Jacobite general at Preston in 1715, spent much of his life at Bamburgh. In 1722 Lord Crewe died and it passed to a charity administered by Dr Sharp, who set up a school and a lifeboat station there, restoring the building with his own money. Over a hundred years later the charity continued until the first Lord Armstrong of Vickers Armstrong took over the property and the ruins were restored to contain eight flats for public tenants, two for staff and accommodation for the Armstrongs. No other British castle, with the exception of Windsor, houses so many people.
Lord Armstrong. Open Easter to October.

Bywell

Close to Prudhoe but on the other side of the Tyne, Bywell is a fifteenth-century tower, built by the Nevilles as the gatehouse to a castle never completed. Part of a curtain wall goes to the old gun house, which has been modernised. There was a Roman bridge over the river here but the castle was not built to defend a river crossing.
Duke of Portland. Not open to the public.

Callaly

The first castle was built in the reign of Henry II and was sited 600 yards (550 m) north-east of the present building but the lady of the house determined to have it in the more sheltered valley. The house is seventeenth-century with nineteenth-century additions, and the south-west tower is a fifteenth-century peel tower. This was built by the Claverings, a Royalist family, who in 1715 fought for the Jacobites at Preston. There is a portrait of General Forster, the inexperienced commander at Preston, in the hall.
Major A. S. C. Browne DL. Open regularly May to mid September.

Cartington
   One of the most unusual and interesting ruins in the county, Cartington stands in farmland 2 miles (3 km) from Rothbury and was probably a thirteenth-century tower but it has been drastically altered. In 1494 it passed to the Radcliffes and during the Civil War it was used as a Royalist armoury. In 1660 it was rebuilt by the Widdringtons, who built the imposing gateway. Further repairs were carried out by Lord Armstrong in Victorian times but now it is very decayed.

Chillingham
   Originally this was a fourteenth-century tower built by Sir Thomas de Heton, added to in the fifteenth century. Now there is a quadrangular house with a deep dungeon in the north-west tower. A famous herd of wild cattle roams the park.
Sir Humphrey Wakefield. House not open to the public. Park open during the summer.

Craster Tower
   Just outside the little port, Craster is a fifteenth-century tower with eighteenth-century additions and still belongs to the Craster family.
Open to the public by written permission only.

Dunstanburgh
   The site of Dunstanburgh belonged to the barony of Embleton and in the thirteenth century to Simon de Montfort. At his death it passed to the Earls of Lancaster, and Thomas, the second Earl, who became High Steward of England, built the castle. In 1313 work was started and the licence was granted three years later, when most of it was finished.
   Earl Thomas was beheaded at Pontefract after the battle of Boroughbridge in 1322 and the castle passed in 1384 to Henry, Duke of Lancaster, and then to his granddaughter Blanche, John of Gaunt's wife. John altered the great gatehouse, which was blocked and turned into a keep. The new entrance on the south-west had a mantlet and additional tower with a drawbridge as extra protection. The inner ward was made at the same time.
   Dunstanburgh became a Lancastrian stronghold during the Wars of the Roses and sheltered many who escaped from the great defeat at Towton. After the Lancastrian defeat at the battle of Hexham in 1464 the castle surrendered to the Earl of Warwick, who occupied it for Edward IV. It was repaired in 1436 and again in 1470, but in 1524 the lead was stripped off and used to repair the castle at Wark-on-Tweed because the Scots could bypass Dunstanburgh but Wark, being on the border, was more important. Elizabeth I had Dunstanburgh surveyed but

decided it was not worth repairing and for many years it belonged to the Earls of Tankerville before becoming ministry property.
English Heritage. Open throughout the year.

Etal

This unusual castle near Norham was crenellated in 1342 and consists of a massive gatehouse and an equally massive keep with a piece of connecting wall. It belonged to the Manners family and was captured by the Scots before Flodden.

Ford

This large quadrangular castle stands on the Till near Etal. William Heron obtained a licence to crenellate his manor at Ford in 1338. It was attacked and burnt by the Scots in 1513 in spite of Lady Heron's efforts to persuade the English commander, the Earl of Surrey, to come to her aid. It must have been efficiently repaired for in 1549 the Scots again attacked it, this time with four guns. The French general Esse was beaten off by young Thomas Carr, son of the governor of Wark, who was besieged in the north-west tower. The young man married a Heron heiress and inherited the castle, much to the resentment of the other Herons. It passed to the Blakes and Delavals and in 1861 it was extensively rebuilt by the Marchioness of Waterford. It is now a field study centre.
Northumberland County Council. Not open to the public.

Harbottle

Inland from Rothbury, the small village of Harbottle on the river Coquet is dominated by the ruin of a large castle. Built by Robert d'Umfraville between 1159 and 1160, it had a shell-keep and two baileys. It was captured by the men of Galloway in 1174. In 1515 it belonged to Lord Dacre, Warden of the Middle March. Queen Margaret, widow of James IV of Scotland, came here with her second husband, the Earl of Angus. Her daughter, born in the castle, was a grandmother of James I of England. In 1584 Harbottle was repaired and the two oillets now visible in the keep probably date from this time. Garrisoned by one hundred soldiers, it was an important Crown fortress commanding the road from Jedburgh over the Cheviots. An extra garrison of part-time soldiers from neighbouring villages could be mustered if required.

Langley

Near Haydon Bridge, Langley Castle is a well restored tower house dating originally from 1350. It was built by Sir Thomas Lucy, one of the commanders at Crecy and Neville's Cross. It was Lancastrian during the Wars of the Roses and Lord Montague captured it in 1464. For a time it belonged to the Radcliffes, but after their involvement in the Jacobite rebellion of 1715 it was settled on Greenwich Hospital. The Governor sold it to a Mr Cadwallader Bates, whose family owns it today.

Langley is oblong in shape with four protruding towers and is now a restaurant.

Lindisfarne

Lindisfarne or Holy Island Castle, a landmark crowning the highest point on the island, was originally a Tudor fort built in 1542, when the harbour was used as an advance base for an expedition against the Scots organised by Lord Hertford. During the early part of the Civil War Captain Rugg held Lindisfarne for the King. It fell into Parliamentary hands in 1645 and when Langdale captured Berwick a strong force was stationed here. In 1675 another fort was built covering the sea approaches.

In 1715 a Jacobite, Laurence Errington, with his nephew captured the fort for one night when only two of the garrison of seven were on duty. The Berwick garrison soon recaptured it and Errington was marched back with his nephew to Berwick jail. Later they escaped, obtained a pardon and opened an inn in Newcastle.

During the Napoleonic Wars Lindisfarne continued to be garrisoned and when the guns were withdrawn in 1819 it became a coastguard station and centre for the Northumberland Artillery Volunteers. In 1902 it was purchased by the owner of *Country Life,* Edward Hudson, who commissioned Edwin Lutyens to turn it into a home. Today it has four living rooms, five bedrooms, an entrance hall and a kitchen. Inside, the simple furniture, much of it designed by Lutyens, makes it one of the most intriguing inhabited castles in England, with a setting second to none.

National Trust. Open regularly April to October. Before visiting the castle, visitors should check the tide timetable in the local newspaper or on the noticeboard at the A1 junction with the road to Beal and Lindisfarne.

Norham

One of the strongest of Northumberland's castles, Norham lies on the Tweed halfway between Wark and Berwick. Part of the Durham palatinate, the castle was built to command the ford and had a constable appointed by the Bishop of Durham. The motte and bailey erected by Bishop Flambard in 1121 were destroyed in two Scottish raids. The existing castle was built by Bishop Hugh in Henry II's reign. It was finished in 1174 and in the same year surrendered to the king, Bishop Hugh being suspected of treason.

In 1215 Alexander II of Scotland besieged it without success. King John visited Norham and in 1217 it was restored to the bishopric. During Edward I's campaign in Scotland, his queen lived here. In 1318 Bishop Lewis appointed Sir Thomas Grey as constable. For a year the castle was under Scottish attack and desperate fighting took place. A Lincolnshire knight, Sir William Marmion, in a spirit of chivalry, charged the Scots single-handed to honour his lady. He was only rescued from death by Grey and others of the garrison who rushed to his help when he was unhorsed.

In Edward III's reign Norham was at last captured by the Scots but did not come to much harm. Soon restored to the bishops, it was repaired and during the Wars of the Roses was besieged by the Lancastrians, holding out only to fall by treachery in 1464. In 1497 Bishop Fox was present during another siege. He was responsible for building the aqueduct and for the water tanks in the moat, which were probably used as an extra water supply.

Shortly before Flodden in 1513 James IV captured Norham with the help of Mons Meg, the mighty cannon of Edinburgh Castle. The castle was repaired and gunners from Portsmouth were added to its garrison. After the Scottish victory at Ancrum Moor in 1545 Norham was immediately repaired and garrisoned by the Earl of Hertford. In 1559 Norham became Crown property and gradually decayed when the borders became peaceful.

The gun ports on the north-west wall are of interest and the arches by the Sheep Gate are very different to any others in the castle. These form the sub-structure of the curtain wall. *English Heritage. Open throughout the year.*

Prudhoe

On the Newcastle to Hexham road, Prudhoe Castle is at Low Prudhoe, near the Tyne. The river course has altered since the castle was built and the steep bank and river formed one solid defensive barrier with a ditch on the other three sides. The stone castle was probably built in the reign of Henry II by Odinel d'Umfraville. In 1174 the Scots failed to take it in a three-day siege. It remained with the d'Umfravilles for nearly four hundred years before passing to the Percys when Henry Percy married the widow of Gilbert d'Umfraville.

The castle is of great interest because of its unusual gatehouse and barbican and its old keep. The main entrance has a chapel above it with an oriel window. The barbican was added in the fourteenth century with a drawbridge and an outer gatehouse; a millpond was sited at the entrance. The nineteenth-century

owner who built the house near to the keep filled in and levelled the outer bailey with several feet of earth.
English Heritage. Open throughout the year.

Seaton Delaval

A Norman castle stood where Sir John Vanbrugh's mansion now stands. Only the chapel remains of the old castle and this has been considerably altered.
Lord Hastings. Open regularly May to September.

Wallington

The Fenwicks had a tower house here, dating from the fourteenth century, but it was destroyed and the foundations are incorporated in Wallington Hall, one of the finest showplaces of Northumberland. The painted hall, depicting incidents in the history of Northumberland, should not be missed.
National Trust. Open April to September, except Tuesdays. Garden open throughout the year.

Warkworth

Near Alnmouth on the river Coquet, Warkworth was once the property of the monks of Lindisfarne. It then passed to the rulers of Northumbria. The castle was built after 1139 by Henry, Earl of Northumberland, son of David I of Scotland. It was in a very weak condition when it was granted by Henry II to Roger Fitzrichard, constable of Newcastle, in recognition of his bravery in a campaign against the Welsh.

His son Robert retained the property on payment of 300 marks to King John in 1199. He built the gatehouse and probably the keep. Robert's son John succeeded in 1214 and on his death in 1240 Roger, the next in line, succeeded. He was killed in a tournament and during the minority of his heir, Robert, Earl of Pembroke, was in charge of the castle. After Robert's death in 1310 his son John of Clavering succeeded. During the war with Scotland in 1322-3 Warkworth held out against Bruce's army but the high cost of equipping the garrison obliged the Claverings to leave and when John died in 1332 the castle passed to Lord Percy of Alnwick. The history of the castle from then on is similar to that of Alnwick.

After the Percy rebellion in 1403 further conspiracy obliged Henry IV to take Warkworth, which he gave to his son John, Duke of Bedford. Henry V restored it to the Percys but the Wars of the Roses saw it pass to Warwick the Kingmaker. Repaired in 1480 it became once more Percy property and the Lion Tower dates from this period. The sixth Earl of Northumberland repaired it, rebuilding the gateway and south wall. He left it to Henry VIII, who granted it to Lord Grey, his Lieutenant of the

Borders. Sir Thomas Percy was restored to Warkworth by Queen Mary in 1557. He took part in the Rising of the North in 1569 and forfeited his property and his head. Warkworth fell into decay and when the Greys of Chillingham owned it in the seventeenth century it ceased to be habitable. The gates were left open and cattle grazed in the bailey. After the Scots occupied it during the Civil War it was demolished by the Percy estate and the stone was used to build a house at Chirton.

The fourth Duke of Northumberland restored the keep in the nineteenth century and today the look-out tower is still in good condition but it is not open to the public. Warkworth is a maze of complicated buildings and the visitor needs a plan to understand them. The medieval bridge and the Hermitage nearby should also be visited.

English Heritage. Open throughout the year.

NORTH YORKSHIRE

Bolton

4 miles (6 km) from Middleham, Bolton is the fourteenth-century castle home of the Scropes. Lord Scrope was Richard II's Lord Chancellor and obtained a licence to crenellate his house in 1379. The work cost 1,000 marks and took eighteen years to complete. The castle has one entrance from the east, a quadrangular courtyard and four towers, one of which collapsed in 1649. As the castle had no moat or outbuildings the defenders had to rely entirely on the strength of the fabric.

Lord Scrope left three sons: the Earl of Wiltshire, who was executed at Bristol in 1399 for treason; Stephen, the Deputy Lieutenant of Ireland; and Roger, who inherited the castle but died shortly after his father. During the Wars of the Roses the Scropes supported the Yorkist cause. In 1513 Henry, ninth Lord Scrope, fought with distinction at Flodden. After her defeat at Langside in 1568, Mary, Queen of Scots, was brought to Bolton for about six months before being moved to Tutbury.

During the Civil War Bolton held out under the twenty-year-old John Scrope. The defenders surrendered after a year's resistance (they had been reduced to eating their horses) and young Scrope was fined and taken to London, where he died. The castle was slighted and does not appear to have been inhabited since. There is a restaurant in the Great Hall.

Hon. Harry Orde-Powlett. Open March to October daily; November to February, tours by arrangement.

Gilling

On a hill beside B1363 between York and Helmsley is Gilling Castle, now a school. It was once a Norman castle belonging to

Roger de Mowbray. At the end of the twelfth century it belonged to the de Etton family and in the reign of Edward II Thomas de Etton constructed a fortified house with a large square tower that forms the base of the present structure. In Henry VII's reign Thomas Fairfax married Elizabeth Etton and Gilling passed to the Fairfaxes. It was Sir William Fairfax who built the famous Jacobean chamber with its wooden panelling, heraldic glass dating from 1585 and a frieze incorporating the arms of local gentry and the twenty-one wapentakes of Yorkshire.

Ampleforth Abbey Trustees. Hall and Great Chamber open daily throughout the year but may be locked at weekends during the school holidays. Gardens open July and August.

Helmsley

Helmsley Castle, on the road between Thirsk and Scarborough, is large and, in its complexities of ditch and rampart, could be called a Yorkshire Caerphilly. After the Conquest Helmsley was granted to Robert de Mortain, half-brother of the Conqueror. William Rufus confiscated the lands in 1088 after the barons' uprising and granted them to William l'Espec. In 1154 Helmsley passed by marriage to the de Roos family and between 1186 and 1227 the present castle walls and three towers were built. The barbican was added in the thirteenth century. At the end of the sixteenth century, Edward Manners, Earl of Rutland, added the oak panelling in the living quarters, some of which survives.

The castle was fortified for the king in 1644 after Marston Moor. It held out for three months against Fairfax, who was wounded and forced to retire to York. Colonel Jordan Crosland finally surrendered on 22nd November 1644 and the castle was slighted. After the Restoration it was claimed by the Duke of Buckingham, whose father had inherited it shortly before his death. The Duke lost his money and died penniless in Kirbymoorside in 1688, and the castle was sold to a London banker, Sir Charles Duncombe, for £95,000. In 1718 Duncombe Park was built nearby.

'Helmsley, once proud Buckingham's delight,
  Slid to a scrivener and a City Knight.'
English Heritage. Open throughout the year.

Knaresborough

Once a Saxon stronghold, Knaresborough was granted by William I to Serlo de Burgh, whose grandson Eustace Fitzjohn built the castle but lived mostly at his other, more magnificent castle at Alnwick. Knaresborough sheltered three of the Becket murderers for a time in 1170, for one of them, Hugh de Morville, was the constable; later the unfortunate Richard II was brought here on his way to Pontefract from Flint. Apart from a twelfth-century pillar all the ruins date from the fourteenth century, when the eleven-towered castle belonged to John of Gaunt.

During the Civil War Knaresborough was a Royalist stronghold; with the Nidd on three sides and a 30 foot (9 m) wall on the other, it proved a difficult fortress for the Parliamentarians to capture. The Royalists surrendered when they ran out of supplies and the castle was slighted in 1648. Cromwell had a particular reason for demolishing it thoroughly, as his son was killed in a skirmish outside its walls.

The large rectangular keep is almost all that remains and the grounds contain the Court House Museum.

Harrogate Borough Council. Keep open Easter to September.

Markenfield

This is one of the oldest and most beautiful of inhabited castles and is on the road between Harrogate and Ripon. It was crenellated in 1311 by John de Markenfield. The Markenfields forfeited their estates for their part in the Rising of the North, in which Richard Norton, uncle of young Markenfield, was the standard-bearer. The castle has a chapel and great hall, which was partly rebuilt by the Egertons in Elizabethan times. In the mid eighteenth century the house was bought back by the family (Fletcher Norton, Lord Grantley). The moat is still complete.

Lord Grantley, MC. Open April to October, Mondays only (exterior open daily in May).

Middleham

The home of Warwick the Kingmaker, Middleham is one of the most famous castles in England. It stands at the entrance to Wensleydale on A6108. The builder of Richmond Castle, the Count of Penhievre, gave the land to his son Alan, who passed it to his brother Ranulph. His grandson Ralph Fitzranulph built the first keep in 1170. When he died his daughter married Robert Neville of Raby. Richard Neville, Earl of Warwick, lived here in the stormy years of the Wars of the Roses and Edward IV was imprisoned here for a short period. After Warwick's death at the battle of Barnet in 1471 the castle was given to Richard, Duke of Gloucester. After the battle of Bosworth Middleham became Crown property until James I gave it to Henry Lindley in 1604. During the Civil War it was slighted by the Roundheads. Thereafter it passed through several hands before becoming the property of the Commissioners of Works in 1925.

The first castle at Middleham was a motte and bailey 500 yards (460 m) south-west of the existing ruin. The curtain walls date from the end of the twelfth century. The rectangular keep, one of the largest in England, originally had corner towers and battlements and a first-floor entrance. Unusually, it incorporates the great hall. The gatehouse is to the north-east and the round Prince's Tower to the south-west. The castle had a moat, most of which has now vanished, and an east bailey.

English Heritage. Open throughout the year.

Pickering

The ruins of Pickering Castle stand on a hill above the river. The first records indicate that the building took place between 1179 and 1180 and most English sovereigns between 1100 and 1400 visited Pickering to hunt wild boar and deer. In 1267 the castle passed to Edmund Crouchback, son of Henry III and Earl of Lancaster. His son, Thomas, was created Steward of England in 1308 and became virtual ruler of the kingdom after Edward II's disastrous engagement at Bannockburn. However, Edward struck back and defeated the barons at Boroughbridge in 1322. Thomas was executed at Pontefract, and the king took possession of the castle. However, after Edward's death in 1327 the castle returned to the family of Lancaster. When Henry Bolingbroke landed at Ravenspur in 1399 he came to Pickering, where he gathered troops to march against Richard II, who was imprisoned here before his removal to Pontefract. The castle belonged to the Duchy of Lancaster until recent times. It was damaged by Roundheads during the Civil War, notably in the west wall, where a breach was made by a battery on the other side of the moat.

The towers date from Edward II's reign and are known as the Mill, Diate Hill, Coleman and Rosamund's towers. The last is of three storeys and is mistakenly named since 'Fair Rosamund', daughter of Lord Clifford and mistress of Henry II, died more than a century before the tower was built in 1323. The keep is shell type and stands on an artificial motte with the inner bailey wall running down from it.

English Heritage. Open throughout the year.

Richmond

The Count of Penhievre began the castle of Richmond in 1071. As a relative of the Duke of Brittany, he owed allegiance to both the King of France and the King of England. He was succeeded by his two brothers and then by his nephew Alan, who married the daughter of the Duke of Brittany, so that in 1146 the new Duke of Brittany, Conan, was the owner of Richmond. He is supposed to have built the keep, one of the finest in the north of England and in appearance somewhat similar to Portchester. Conan's daughter was betrothed to

Geoffrey, son of Henry II, who took over the dukedom and the castle. Their son Arthur was murdered by agents of King John in 1203 and the castle, after a spell as a possession of the Earl of Leicester, passed to the Crown. After further changes of ownership Richard II gave the castle to his queen, Anne of Bohemia, and Henry Bolingbroke gave it to the Nevilles. From 1453 to 1456 it went to Henry VI's half-brother, Edmund Tudor, whose son became Henry VII. The Earls of Lennox became Dukes of Richmond in 1601 and the castle remained their property until it passed to the Ministry of Works.

Richmond covers a large area and Scolland's Hall in the south corner is one of the earliest surviving Norman halls, with an outside stair leading to the first floor. The keep, once the entrance to the castle, dates from 1150. Most of the remains are eleventh- or twelfth-century. Richmond was in ruins by the sixteenth century.

English Heritage. Open throughout the year.

Ripley

Ripley Castle is on the road from Ripon to Harrogate and dates mostly from the sixteenth century although the gatehouse is believed to have been built in 1418. It was once a tower house. The Ingilbys have lived here for six hundred years. According to tradition Thomas de Ingilby saved Edward III from a wild boar and was granted free hunting in Knaresborough Forest and later the right to hold a market in Ripley. The family supported the Royalist cause during the Civil War and raised a troop of horse which fought at Marston Moor, Jane Ingilby accompanying them dressed as a trooper. During their absence Cromwell spent a night at Ripley, sitting with Lady Ingilby, who had a pair of pistols in her apron. The castle was rebuilt in 1780 and the village was replanned by Sir William Amcotts in 1827, modelled on a village in Alsace.

Sir T. Ingilby, Bt. Open regularly, Easter to October.

Scarborough

Once a Roman signal station and before that the site of a bronze age dwelling, the castle was built by William Le Gros, Lord of Holderness, in about 1136. It had a moat protecting the curtain on the harbour side and an extended barbican covering the main entrance. After William's death in 1179 at Bytham (Lincolnshire) Henry II took over Scarborough and built the keep, which, with its external steps, is reminiscent of Hedingham in Essex. Once this was 100 feet (30 m) high but half of it was demolished in 1649.

In 1312 Piers Gaveston, favourite of Edward II, was besieged here and surrendered to the Earl of Pembroke. In 1536 during the Pilgrimage of Grace the castle resisted the cannon of Sir Robert Aske for three weeks. In 1553 Thomas Stafford captured the castle for three days by a trick. He took thirty friends disguised as peasants into the bailey. They seized the guards at the main gate and let in armed retainers. The Earl of Westmorland recaptured it for Queen Mary; Stafford and four of his associates were executed.

During the Civil War the port of Scarborough was vital to the Royalist cause and Sir Hugh Cholmley held the castle for the king against Meldrum's troops. Cannon were placed in St Mary's church but the Royalists destroyed the chancel with accurate gunfire from the ramparts. Meldrum was mortally wounded and Matthew Boynton took command. Cholmley surrendered on 22nd July 1645, the garrison marching out in good order. In 1648 the garrison again declared for the king, and the leader of the revolt, another Boynton (no relation to Matthew), held out until December before surrendering. He escaped to play a noble part in the Preston campaign, finally being killed at Wigan in August 1648.

In the eighteenth century the castle was used as an ammunition dump and a new barracks was built in the bailey. In 1914 the German battleships *Derfflinger* and *Van der Tann* fired salvoes into the town and castle, demolishing the barracks.

English Heritage. Open throughout the year.

Sheriff Hutton

This is one of the most spectacular ruins in Yorkshire. The original castle was built by Bertram de Bulmer about 1140 and was a keep and bailey with a large earth wall. In 1379 Lord Neville of Raby built a large four-towered castle, similar to Bolton. Each tower had four storeys. Elizabeth of York, wife of Henry VII, lived here for a time and it later belonged to Henry Fitzroy, illegitimate son of Henry VIII. By the seventeenth century it was in ruins and Charles I gave orders for it to be partially demolished. The gatehouse has a frieze with four shields and there are remains of the moat, which was double on the south side.

Unrestricted access.

Skipton

A timber castle was probably erected at Skipton after the Norman conquest but Robert de Romille soon replaced it in stone. About 1100 it passed to William de Fortibus, whose successors, Earls of Albemarle, held it until 1245, when it became Crown property, as it did several times in the next 250 years. In 1310 Robert Clifford began his family's long association with Skipton when he became first Lord of the Honour of

Skipton. He built the four drum towers on the south side and the massive four-towered gatehouse. He was killed at Bannockburn. The tenth Lord Henry, Clifford, the 'Shepherd Lord', commanded the English in their rout of the Scots at Flodden in 1513. He constructed a Tudor residence inside the castle, incorporated into the Conduit Court; the Long Gallery was added later.

In the Civil War Sir John Mallory held the castle for Charles I and withstood siege for three years before surrendering on generous terms in 1645. The castle was slighted but restored soon afterwards by Lady Anne Clifford. It is now in excellent condition and the Conduit Court is renowned for its beauty. *Thomas Fattorini Limited. Open throughout the year.*

Spofforth

Near Wetherby, Spofforth Castle can only just be seen from the road and only a third of it remains today. It was a thirteenth-century fortified manor of the Percy family, whose main residences were at Wressle and Topcliffe. In 1408 Henry Percy, first Earl of Northumberland, was killed at Bramham Moor in a rebellion against Henry IV. Henry Hotspur, his son, who was born at the castle, had been killed at Shrewsbury in 1403 and the third Earl was killed with his brother fighting for the Lancastrians at Towton in 1461.

The castle is rectangular and today consists of a great hall and an undercroft. There is a particularly fine two-light west window that once belonged to the solar.
English Heritage. Open throughout the year.

York

York originally had two mottes. One is now Bail Hill and the other, across the river, is all that remains of the castle — the remarkable Clifford's Tower. In 1190 the Jews of York were massacred on the hill. The wooden tower was burned but replaced at once with another timber tower; the rebuilding in stone began in 1245 and was substantially complete in 1272. It has a quatrefoil plan consisting of four intersected towers each with a radius of 22 feet (6.7 m). The arms of the Clifford family, below royal arms, are over the entrance. The tower possibly derives its name from the hanging in chains from its summit of Roger de Clifford after the Royalists had defeated the rebels at Boroughbridge in 1322. In 1684 it was blown up accidentally and many of the soldiers inside were killed. In 1825 it was repaired and a jail was built in the bailey where the Castle Museum stands today.
English Heritage. Open throughout the year. York Castle Museum opposite open throughout the year.

NOTTINGHAMSHIRE
Newark

One of the most important castles in the Midlands, Newark-on-Trent lies on the Roman Fosse Way and on the medieval Great North Road where it crosses the Trent. The castle that stands today was built by Alexander, Bishop of Lincoln, who also built Banbury and Sleaford castles.

King John held the castle until the close of his reign, when it was seized by the barons. In October 1216, the weary king spent the last three days of his life here. When he died his body was moved, as he wished, to Worcester, where his monument stands in the cathedral. The barons held the castle against Henry III and for eight days Lord Pembroke battered it with his siege engines before it surrendered. In 1480 Bishop Rotherham altered the Great Hall, adding an oriel window, and in 1547 the castle reverted to the Crown. Later it was leased to Sir Francis Leeke at an annual rent of 53s 4d. James I stopped here on his way to take over the throne of England and was so horrified at the state of the prisoners that he freed them all.

During the Civil War the town of Newark was a Royalist stronghold. Well defended by the rivers Trent and Devon, with the earthwork cannon platforms known as the King's Sconce and the Queen's Sconce protecting the Fosse Way, it was a difficult position to attack. The first siege was beaten off in 1643 but in 1644 Sir John Meldrum arrived with a force of over eight thousand men. Prince Rupert with six thousand men came to the rescue in the early hours of 21st March and, before all his men had arrived, attacked the Parliamentary horse on Beacon Hill. Meldrum moved into the 'island' and Sir Richard Byron attacked him across the river from the castle. Surprised, and alarmed at his lack of provisions, Meldrum surrendered. A further Parliamentary attack was defeated by Langdale's Horse and after Naseby Charles came to Newark twice, for it was his only safe refuge in the region. On the second occasion there occurred the quarrel with Prince Rupert after which the Prince virtually ceased to play any further part in the struggle. John Belasyse, the new governor of the castle, held out against the Scots under Leslie, as well as against the English, until May 1646, when he was ordered to surrender by Charles himself. The king had walked into the Scots camp at Kelham and no one was more surprised at the command than the unfortunate Belasyse, a veteran of Edgehill, who escaped to France, where he was killed in a drunken brawl.

The castle's north gateway dating from 1170 is the largest of any castle in England. In the north end of the structure is an undercroft which was below the state apartments. Today Newark Castle is seen best from the Trent bridge for, although

slighted in 1646, the ruins are well preserved.
Newark District Council. Grounds open at all reasonable times.
Display in south-west tower has limited opening times.

Nottingham

The castle today is very different from the medieval building. It was built by William I in 1068 above the river Leen and in the late fifteenth century had three baileys with three gateways and two large towers. The keep was built in 1213, as were numerous smaller towers and living quarters. Medieval features that survive include the outer bailey gatehouse and bridge, the middle bailey bridge, part of the middle and outer bailey curtain walls and fragments of Richard's Tower.

King John called it his favourite castle but the event for which the castle is best known occurred in 1330. Three years before this Mortimer and Queen Isabella had contrived the murder of Edward II at Berkeley Castle. Edward III, urged by his supporters to dispose of Mortimer, organised a party with Sir William Eland, the deputy constable, and a few others to enter the castle at night, possibly by way of an underground passage known as Mortimer's Hole. Mortimer was dragged out of his chamber in the inner ward and taken to London, where he was given a mock trial and hanged at Tyburn. Mortimer's Hole, still visible today, is one of an elaborate series of tunnels leading through the castle rock.

Richard III raised his army here against Henry Tudor and in 1642 the Royalist standard of Charles I was raised on a hill to the north of the castle. The street is now called Standard Hill Street. The weather was bad and the wind blew the flag down during the night, which many considered an ill omen for the war. From 1643 Colonel Hutchinson was the Parliamentary governor in the 'very ruinous and uninhabitable' castle, and his wife, Lady Hutchinson, wrote the memoirs which have become famous. After the war Colonel Hutchinson instigated the demolition of the structure and the Duke of Newcastle, who acquired the site, built an Italian style house. This was burnt during the Reform Bill riots in 1831. The castle now houses the Castle Museum and the Sherwood Foresters Regimental Museum.
Nottingham City Council. Open throughout the year.

OXFORDSHIRE

Broughton

Broughton Castle, 3 miles (5 km) west of Banbury, stands on an island surrounded by a broad moat. The original house, of which much remains, was built by John de Broughton in about 1300. The house was purchased by William of Wykeham in 1377 and his nephew Thomas later obtained a licence to crenellate and built the impressive gatehouse and the adjoining battlements. In 1450 Margaret Wykeham married James, first Lord Saye and Sele, whose family have owned and lived at Broughton ever since. In the sixteenth century the house was greatly enlarged and embellished with elaborate plaster ceilings, panelled rooms and many fine fireplaces.

The most famous Lord Saye and Sele was William, one of the leaders of the Parliamentarians in the years preceding the Civil War. In the room at the top of the house known as the Council Chamber, secret meetings were held, attended by fellow Parliamentarians including Pym, John Hampden, Sir John Eliot, Lord Brook and Henry Vane. Lord Saye and Sele and his four sons were all present at the Battle of Edgehill but had moved elsewhere when Broughton was besieged and captured by the Royalist forces on the next day. At the restoration of Charles II in 1660 Lord Saye and Sele was pardoned and honoured by being made Lord Privy Seal. His son Nathaniel Fiennes, whose portrait in a buff coat and armour hangs in the Great Hall, was the Parliamentary colonel in charge at the siege of Bristol and condemned to death for surrendering to Prince Rupert. His daughter Celia is remembered for the account of her journeys round England on horseback, a book that provides one of the best descriptions of life at the end of the seventeenth century. *The Lord Saye and Sele. Open Wednesdays and Sundays, mid May to mid September, also Thursdays in July and August and Bank holiday Sundays and Mondays.*

Minster Lovell

One of the most picturesque ruins in the county, Minster Lovell Hall and church lie on the banks of the Windrush just off A40 between Witney and Burford. The manor was granted to William Lovell by his mother Maud in about 1180 and later the church was given to Ivrey Abbey, thus becoming a small priory.

The Lovells seem to have been soldiers for three centuries. William was one of the English knights in the Third Crusade. In the thirteenth century John Lovell was Marshal of the Army in Scotland. His son was killed at Bannockburn. In 1408 John, the sixth Lord Lovell, inherited Minster Lovell and on his death it passed to his son William, who obtained possession in 1423 on the death of his grandmother. These Lovells were wealthy and William built the hall on his return from the French wars in about 1435. The south-west tower and river wall make it a fortified manor and were added in the fifteenth century.

William Lovell, whose tomb can be seen in the church, was a Lancastrian, but his son Francis, the last and most famous of the Lovells, was a Yorkist. He was a man of some ability and during the reign of Richard III he became a viscount, Chamberlain of the Household and Constable of Wallingford Castle. A contemporary saying went: 'The cat, the rat and Lovell our dog ruled all England under the Hog'.

At Bosworth Lovell was one of the few Yorkist leaders to escape with his life. He fled to Flanders but returned a year later with Lambert Simnel. At Stoke, near Newark, their army was defeated by the Earl of Oxford and Henry VII. Lovell was last seen swimming his horse over the Trent. His death was a mystery until 1708 when some workmen erecting a new chimney on the hall found a large vault. A letter of 1737 written to Francis Peck, a local historian, describes the scene: 'where was the skeleton of a man . . . sitting at a table which was before him with a book, paper, pen, etc; in another part of the room lay a cap all moulded and decayed. Which the family took to be this Lord Lovell whose exit hath hitherto been so uncertain.'

The manor went to the Crown until 1602, when it was purchased by Sir Edward Coke. Thomas Coke, Earl of Leicester, lived here for a time but in 1734, when his new house had been built at Holkham in Norfolk, the hall fell into decay. It was finally demolished in 1747 and a print of 1775 shows it in much the same state as it is today.

English Heritage. Open throughout the year.

Oxford

In New Road near the railway station is the rectangular keep of Oxford Castle. Built by Robert d'Oyley it was once used as a prison and originally had four towers. Queen Matilda, dressed in white, escaped from here with three companions by walking over the frozen river to Abingdon.

Shirburn

Near the pleasant old town of Watlington and just off B4009, Shirburn is one of the few inhabited small castles in England. The castle came into the possession of Warine de l'Isle, who obtained a licence to crenellate and built the present building in 1378. When he died, his granddaughter inherited the estate and she married the twelfth Earl of Warwick. In 1426, however, it was in the possession of a local family, the Quatremaynes of Thame. Richard Quatremayne left it to his servant Thomas Fowler, but the Fowlers were always in debt and Richard Fowler married his daughter Sibyl to Richard Chamberlain, giving them Shirburn in exchange for enough money to pay his creditors.

During the Civil War Shirburn escaped destruction due to the common sense of the Chamberlains, who were Royalists, but remained neutral. One of the Chamberlains married a Gage and in 1716 it was sold to Lord Parker, Lord Chief Justice, who was created Earl of Macclesfield by George I. The same family owns it today.

Built of brick originally, in the nineteenth century the castle was covered in plaster stucco. The windows were modernised and a drawbridge was built over the wide moat.

The Earl of Macclesfield. Not open to the public.

SHROPSHIRE

Acton Burnell

About 4 miles (6 km) from Shrewsbury towards Wenlock Edge is the small village of Acton Burnell with its four-sided ruined castle standing next to the church. It was built by Edward I's Lord Chancellor, Edward Burnell, who was Bishop of Bath and Wells. King Edward came here in 1283 and it was in the great barn, the gable ends of which still remain, that the first Parliament was held, when the Statute of Acton Burnell was passed dealing with the collection of business debts.

The castle was built the following year of red sandstone. Acton Burnell is one of the earliest fortified mansions in the country and was never built to withstand a siege.

After the death of Bishop Burnell the family lived here until the marriage of Maud Burnell with John Lovell in 1315. Their famous descendant was Francis, Lord Lovell (see Minster Lovell, Oxfordshire). Henry VII acquired the castle in 1486 after the battle of Stoke and Henry VIII presented it to the Earl of Surrey for his services in leading the successful Flodden campaign. During the reign of Charles II, Sir Richard Lee's heiress married Sir Edward Smythe and the Smythe family still owns the property today.

Open to the public.

Bridgnorth

Earl Robert de Belleme, a Norman baron and a supporter of Robert, brother of Henry I, built the castle at Bridgnorth on the edge of a cliff. The keep, which stands today at an angle of 17 degrees, was erected 'in a great hurrey' by Henry II. Henry granted Bridgnorth to Hugh de Mortimer, who later supported Stephen. Henry besieged the castle when Mortimer held out for Stephen and one of his archers nearly killed the king: only the quick action of Hubert St Clair saved Henry. He jumped in front of the king and thereby lost his own life. The castle became Crown property and Edward II was captured here by Roger Mortimer.

During the Civil War Colonel Howard garrisoned Bridgnorth for the King and in 1646 the castle was besieged for three weeks. Mines were driven through the cliff and Howard, running out of ammunition, was forced to surrender. The castle was slighted and the keep, undermined, toppled to its present extraordinary position. Lavington's Hole, as the mine is called, is still visible and when it was explored at the beginning of the twentieth century some old candles were discovered.

The entrance to the grounds is at the end of West Castle Street on the right of St Mary's church, which once stood within the bailey.

Bridgnorth Town Council. Open throughout the year.

Clun

On A488 near the Herefordshire border are the remains of the twelfth-century castle of the de Says, who were granted the land by Roger de Montgomery, Earl of Shrewsbury. Clun has three baileys connected by narrow causeways and on the motte are a rectangular keep and two semicircular towers. The river acts as a moat to what must have been a formidable fortress.

In the town hall, once the castle court house, is a small museum.

Museum open Easter to November. Unrestricted access to ruins.

Ludlow

Built by Roger de Lacy in 1086, Ludlow is the principal castle of the thirty-two that guarded the Welsh Marches. Roger de Lacy was exiled after rebelling against William Rufus and the property passed to his brother and, on the latter's death, to the Crown.

During the reign of Henry I Ludlow was granted to Pain Fitzjohn, who was killed by the Welsh in 1136. The round chapel in the inner bailey dates from 1120. In 1138 Gervase de Paganel captured Ludlow on behalf of Queen Matilda and in the ensuing siege King Stephen saved the young Prince Henry of Scotland from being dragged off his horse by a grappling iron. The window from which the iron was thrown is still pointed out today.

Pain's successor, Joyce de Dinan, was virtually a prisoner in his own castle after 1150, when de Paganel was ousted. Hugh de Mortimer threatened him and Joyce, by a clever ambush, captured Hugh and imprisoned him in a tower in the outer bailey, ever since called Mortimer's Tower. Mortimer obtained his freedom by paying 3,000 marks in ransom. In 1166 Joyce died and the castle was seized by Hugh de Lacy. King John then acquired it for himself until restoring it eventually to Hugh's brother, Walter de Lacy. This was a period of incessant war against the Welsh, and Ludlow remained fully garrisoned. The de Genevilles, relations of the de Lacys, inherited the property and Joan de Geneville married Roger Mortimer, first Earl of March and virtual ruler of England during the minority of

Edward III. During the Wars of the Roses Ludlow was the property of Richard, Duke of York, who was nephew to the fifth Earl of March. The battle of Ludford Bridge was fought over the Teme when Henry VI and his army closed in on Ludlow and Richard decided to attack the Lancastrians early in the morning before they had time to get to arms. His scheme was foiled, however, by the treachery of Sir Andrew Trollope, who deserted Richard in the night and took his experienced troops over to Henry's side, forcing York to flee to Ireland. The castle was sacked and the Lancastrians were in temporary command until the position was reversed at the battle of Northampton in 1460.

From 1472 to 1483 the young Prince of Wales and his brother lived in the castle until they went to London and eventually met their death in the Tower. Edward IV had instituted a prince's council in Ludlow for administering justice in Wales. This Court of the Marches was carried on by Henry VII, whose son Arthur lived at Ludlow. Under Elizabeth I Sir Henry Sidney was governor for twenty-seven years. He built the gatehouse (inscribed 1581) into the middle ward and repaired the keep, which was used as a prison. The Court of the Marches continued until 1689, when it was abolished by William III, and the castle thereafter declined in importance.

Milton's *Comus* was first performed at Ludlow and Butler wrote *Hudibras* in a room over the gateway. The building was not seriously damaged during the Civil War, when it was mostly held by the Royalists. It was during the reign of George I that it suffered most, when the lead was stripped off the roof of the main hall, bringing about the decay of what was once one of England's proudest castles.

Powis Estates. Open February to November.

Moreton Corbet

North of Shrewsbury off A53, the ruins of the Elizabethan manor stand close to the older ruins of the castle. It is believed to have been built by the Turret family in the late twelfth century. One of the Turret heiresses married Richard Corbet of Wattlesborough. Roger Corbet, who had travelled in Italy, built the Elizabethan house in 1579. It was never completed, as Corbet died of the plague, and his cousin Sir Richard did not live much longer, dying in 1606. Sir Vincent Corbet, who succeeded, was an ardent Royalist and garrisoned the castle with eighty foot soldiers and thirty horsemen. The Parliamentary army at Wem, commanded by Colonel Rinking, attacked the castle during the night and captured it. The roof was removed and when the Corbets regained their property they moved to Shawbury Park, so the castle and its magnificent Elizabethan house fell rapidly into ruins. The Corbet crest, an elephant and castle, can be seen on the screen in the church. Moreton ranks with Kirby Hall, Northamptonshire, as one of the finest Elizabethan architectural ruins in the country.

English Heritage. Open throughout the year.

Shrewsbury

Roger de Montgomery built Shrewsbury Castle on a loop of the Severn in about 1080. Roger's successor extended the walls to the other side of the river and in the twelfth century the town walls were built.

In 1138 Shrewsbury was besieged by Stephen and captured after four weeks of resistance. The entire garrison was hanged, except William Fitzalan, the owner, who escaped. Henry II used Shrewsbury, now a royal castle, as a springboard for his attacks against the Welsh. Henry IV garrisoned the castle against Hotspur before the battle of Shrewsbury in 1403, when young Prince Hal helped his father defeat the rebel army.

During the Civil War Shrewsbury was an important Royalist training centre. In February 1645 Colonels Boyer and Mytton with 1,200 Parliamentary troops attacked it at night and, with the loss of only two men, took it by climbing over the east wall.

In the eighteenth century the crumbling ruin was bought by Sir William Pulteney MP, who wanted a town house large enough for receptions. His architect was Thomas Telford, who carried out many repairs. Further modernisation was carried out by Sir Charles Nicholson in 1926. Today it is well looked after and the grounds are a park and garden.

Open throughout the year.

Stokesay

Stokesay lies in a secluded position not far from Craven Arms. It was the Norman home of the de Say family — hence the name (the word 'stoke' means dairy farm) — and the castle was rebuilt by Lawrence Ludlow, a wool merchant, who obtained a licence to crenellate in 1291. The great hall is of cruck construction and the timber markings are still visible. There used to be an open fire in the centre of the floor and the black timbers are an indication that the usual louvres in the roof to let out the smoke never existed.

In 1497 Anne Ludlow married Thomas Vernon and their family lived here until the sixteenth century, when Stokesay was sold to Sir George Mainwaring. Later it was sold to Dame Elizabeth Craven and her son, the Royalist Lord Craven but they never lived here. The castle surrendered to Parliament in 1645 and most of the curtain wall was reduced in height. Stokesay was leased to the Baldwyns in 1648 and they made many alterations before subletting it about 1728. By 1814, it was rapidly becoming a ruin. Lord Craven added the hall buttresses and in 1869 Stokesay was sold for the fifth time. The new owner, Mr J. D. Allcroft, preserved it and the present owner, his granddaughter, has carried on with the work, still incomplete. *Sir Philip and Lady Magnus-Allcroft. Open March to October, daily except Tuesdays; November, weekends only.*

Upton Cressett

Near Bridgnorth is the medieval and Elizabethan home of the de Upton and Cressett families with its fine brick chimneys and gatehouse. The house was once surrounded by a moat and there is evidence of a drawbridge between gatehouse and manor. Today it is a private house. In the Wars of the Roses Hugh Cressett, a Lancastrian, lived here and young Edward V was said to have stayed here on his way to the Tower of London. Richard Cressett supplied money to fight the Spanish Armada and Edward was a Royalist leader during the Civil War. He was killed at Bridgnorth in 1646 and his son Francis plotted to rescue the king from Carisbrooke.
Mr W. Cash. Open May to October, Thursdays only.

Whittington

2 miles (3 km) to the east of Oswestry, the gatehouse, ditch and tower stand on a bend of A5 by the railway line. Fulk de Warenne paid Henry III £262 and two chargers for the manor with a licence to crenellate it in 1219. Recent clearance and excavation have laid bare the foundations of a rectangular tower keep surrounded by curtain walls with round corner towers. The gatehouse fronting the A5 led into a small outer courtyard, from which a drawbridge led over a wet moat to a now much damaged twin-towered inner gateway. The remains are now laid out as a public open space.

SOMERSET

Castle Neroche

In the Blackdown Hills not far from the village of Buckland St Mary, Neroche is a collection of three banks and ditches. The inner one is the largest and has an entrance leading to a farm. The motte to the north is from a twelth-century motte and bailey castle built on the site of a much earlier hillfort.
Forestry Commission. Nature trail and picnic area. Unrestricted access.

Dunster

Just outside Minehead, Dunster Castle stands high on the western edge of Exmoor, dominating the valley and the village. William de Mohun built a castle here on a Saxon site after the Battle of Hastings. The thirteenth-century gateway built by the Mohuns survives. In 1376 the last male heir of the Mohuns died and the castle was sold to Elizabeth Luttrell. Hugh Luttrell built the outer gatehouse in 1420.

The Luttrells were Lancastrians. James was killed at the battle of St Albans in 1461. The next three Luttrells were all knighted. During the Civil War Dunster was besieged twice, first by the Royalists and then by the Parliamentarians. Afterwards most of the fortifications were demolished. George Luttrell took up residence again in 1651 on payment of a fine. During the Monmouth Rebellion some of the Luttrell retainers went to the Duke's support and there is a halberd in the castle supposed to have been made there for use in the rising.

Inside is a magnificent staircase dating from 1681, and the dining room has plasterwork of the same date. The house was remodelled by Salvin in the nineteenth century.
National Trust. Open April to October.

Farleigh Hungerford

On the Wiltshire border, near Trowbridge, Farleigh Hungerford was built by Sir Thomas Hungerford on the site of a small Norman manor belonging to the Montforts. Sir Thomas was Speaker of the House of Commons in 1377 and made money in the war with France. He fortified his manor without a licence but received royal consent later. His son Walter, also Speaker and a soldier, enlarged the outer court of the castle and on his death in 1449 his widow built a chapel.

In 1462 Richard, Duke of Gloucester, gave it to the Duke of Norfolk. But at Bosworth Norfolk was killed and Sir Walter Hungerford regained the family property in 1486. Colonel John Hungerford garrisoned the castle for Charles during the Civil War but later surrendered it to his half-brother, Sir Edward, the last Hungerford to live in the castle. He became a Whig and was involved in the Rye House Plot; this and his spendthrift ways forced him to sell Farleigh to a Mr Baynton, brother-in-law to the Earl of Rochester. In 1730, it was sold again to the Houltons of Trowbridge and remained in their hands until 1891 when it was bought by Lord Donington. Later it was sold to Lord Cairns, who placed it under the guardianship of the Ministry of Works in 1915.

The gatehouse and the chapel are virtually complete and the latter houses an interesting display of armour, mostly of the Civil

War period.
English Heritage. Open throughout the year.

Nunney

John de la Mare obtained a licence to crenellate his house near Frome in 1373. He was interested in French castles and his building is unique amongst English castles. The four towers are very close together and are surmounted by machicolated parapets and round turrets that once had conical roofs. It has a wide deep moat and for two days in 1645 it held out against Fairfax until a 36 pounder cannon knocked down one wall and the garrison under Colonel Prater surrendered. The slighting was inefficiently done and much of the building remains today.
English Heritage. Open throughout the year. Key from caretaker's cottage.

Stogursey

Near Bridgwater, the castle of the de Courcys was held for King John in 1215 and destroyed the following year. A few walls and the moat remain. One of the de Courcys subdued Ulster and became its first Earl. The castle is now restored as a ruin, with a caretaker in the moat cottage.
Landmark Trust.

Taunton

In the centre of the town and now the County Museum, the castle hall was built on a Saxon site by William Gifford between 1107 and 1129. The keep was added by Henry of Blois between 1129 and 1171 and further buildings were added in 1207.

The castle was a ruin by 1490 and had to be repaired by Bishop Langton of Winchester. During the Civil War it was captured and held by Blake for Parliament. The inner moat was filled in by Sir Benjamin Hammet, who carried out other alterations so that Taunton Castle today has lost most of its character.
Somerset County Council. Museum open throughout the year. The Somerset Military Museum is also in the castle.

SOUTH YORKSHIRE

Conisbrough

One of the most important of the Yorkshire castles, Conisbrough is in the middle of an industrial area between Doncaster and Rotherham. The first owner was William de Warenne, Earl of Surrey, who probably erected a wooden structure. In 1163 his grandson's daughter Isabel married Hamelin Plantagenet, the half-brother of Henry II. There is a written reference to an endowment of 50 shillings a year for a chapel in the castle and it is generally presumed that Hamelin built the famous keep with its six massive buttresses rising to 86 feet (26 m). The keep has three chambers, one of which was an oratory.

The castle later belonged to the Duke of York who died at Agincourt and passed to Richard, Duke of York, father of Edward IV and Richard III. After 1446 the castle was neglected and later passed to the Carey family. By the sixteenth century it was so ruinous that during the Civil War it was not fortified and so escaped slighting.

In England there are no other keeps of the same design and one has to go to France to find anything comparable of the same age for example Houdan, Etampes or Chateau Gaillard.

English Heritage. Open throughout the year.

STAFFORDSHIRE

Caverswall

Near Stoke-on-Trent, Caverswall was crenellated in 1275. It has an oblong enclosure and four corner towers, but the house dates from 1615 and was constructed by Robert Smythson for the Cradock family. Fully restored today, with dungeons and moat, Caverswall is not open to the public.

Eccleshall

Between Stafford and Market Drayton, Eccleshall was originally the fortified mansion of the Bishop of Lichfield. In 1459 it was an important Lancastrian stronghold to which Lord Audley's army withdrew after defeat at Blore Heath. Only a tower remains.

The Carter family. Open March to October.

Tamworth

One of the most important Midland castles Tamworth lies just off A5 not far from Lichfield. The shell-keep was built in Norman times by the Marmions. The herringbone stone wall that crosses the moat may date from the reign of Henry I.

The Marmions held Tamworth during the twelfth and thirteenth centuries. The Ferrers of Groby inherited it during the Wars of the Roses and the family lived there for over two hundred years. During the Civil War the owner, John Ferrers, was a minor and the castle escaped serious damage, although it was garrisoned by both Royalists and Parliamentarians.

The castle has a great hall with a magnificent late medieval to early Tudor timbered roof and windows with sixteenth-century glass. There are several fine Jacobean state apartments and a museum.

Tamworth Borough Council. Open throughout the year.

Tutbury

3 miles (5 km) north of Burton on Trent on A50, Tutbury Castle stands on a bend of the Dove and was once a Saxon stronghold. Much of the ruin remains standing although the keep is a sham nineteenth-century structure erected by one of the Vernon family. The castle was originally granted by William I to Henry de Ferrers, later made Earl of Derby, but when a Ferrers supported Simon de Montfort in 1266, the castle was forfeited to the house of Lancaster.

Thomas, second Earl of Lancaster, who lived here in 1322, was driven out by Edward II and lost his treasure in the Dove during his escape. Some of the coins were discovered in 1831 and are now in the British Museum. In 1350 John of Gaunt inherited Tutbury and spent a great sum of money on its repairs, as well as introducing the sport of bull running to the town. Later Tutbury was one of the castles used to imprison Mary, Queen of Scots. She was allowed a retinue of forty-seven people, ten horses and a guard of thirty soldiers. Her custodian, Sir Richard Sadler, took her hawking and was afterwards censured for his kindness.

During the Civil War Tutbury was garrisoned for the king by Lord Loughborough. It surrendered and was reduced to its present state by Brereton in 1646.
Open throughout the year.

SUFFOLK

Bungay

About 12 miles (19 km) west of Lowestoft is the small town of Bungay. It was a natural place for a castle and Roger Bigod, owner of Framlingham, built the first castle here. It was in occupation during Stephen's reign when Hugh Bigod supported the cause of Matilda. The king captured it and made terms with Bigod, but the unrepentant baron later joined the Earl of Leicester's rebellion against Henry II and in 1174 Bungay again came under attack. In 1891 excavations carried out here revealed the mine constructed in 1174. It runs from the west wall to the prison beneath the forebuilding. Another gallery had been started but not finished.
Unrestricted access.

Clare

The Saxons built a large earthwork at Clare (which later became the site of the railway station and is now the centre of Clare Castle Country Park). At the time of the Norman conquest Clare was one of the ninety-five lordships given to Richard Fitzgilbert. Richard's son Gilbert de Clare annexed the little chapel of St John to the Abbey of Bec in Normandy and was probably responsible for building the castle, of which very little stonework remains, although the ramparts and parts of the moat are visible.

Unrestricted access.

Framlingham

Framlingham is probably the most important castle in Suffolk. The town of Framlingham is about 4 miles (6 km) west of A12 at Wickham Market and the castle still presents an impressive aspect. The earliest definite record of the castle is of it being given by Henry I to Roger Bigod about 1100. Roger's second son, Hugh, was created Earl of Norfolk by Stephen and in 1173 joined the Earl of Leicester in his rebellion against Henry II. Henry, returning from France, captured Ipswich, Walton and Bungay castles, all possessions of Hugh, and Framlingham surrendered. It was dismantled and the ditch filled in, but around 1190 the second Earl, Roger II, began construction of the present castle.

Today it consists of three wards, the inner one surrounded by a 44 foot (13.4 m) wall with thirteen towers, mostly intact, surrounded by a moat and the outer bailey, which itself had a moat. To the west was the small lower court protected by an artificial marsh. Roger II built the walls incorporating the chapel and great hall against the eastern curtain between 1190 and 1210. His defensive scheme was copied from the Crusaders' castles based upon the Roman idea of a defensive wall interspaced with towers.

The wall walk, not recommended for those afraid of heights, commands an excellent view of the town and takes one round nine of the thirteen towers. The strange Tudor chimneys, added by the later Howards, are dummies except in the eighth and ninth towers. The drawbridge was of the counterweight variety and the present bridge dates from 1524.

English Heritage. Open throughout the year.

Orford

On the Suffolk coast south of Aldeburgh (but best approached via Woodbridge) stands one of the most unusual castles in England. The keep, which is all that remains, is polygonal on the outside and circular on the inside. It has three square projecting towers and a forebuilding between the south turret and the main structure. According to the Pipe Rolls, which are remarkably complete for this part of Suffolk, Orford Castle was built between 1166 and 1172 by Henry II, when Orford was a busy port on the river Alde, and it was completed in time to put down the rebellion of Hugh Bigod, Earl of Norfolk, who owned the castles of Bungay, Framlingham, Walton and Thetford. Supplied by sea, Orford was a useful base and the revolt was soon crushed. In 1217, during the Barons' War, the French occupied the castle but, although it changed hands on more than one occasion, at no time was the keep damaged and in 1277 two of the towers were further protected by lead roofs.

There are no traces of the bailey walls today. Originally the curtain enceinte had bastions protecting the intermediate walls but the walls gradually vanished, the last piece falling down in 1841. In 1336 Edward III gave it to Robert Ufford, Earl of Suffolk, and it remained in private hands until its presentation to the Ministry of Public Building and Works in 1962.

Inside Orford, reached by a second-storey door as at Hedingham Castle (Essex), there is a large, well lit chamber, with a spiral staircase in one tower and chambers in the others. In the basement is a deep well with a ladder cut into the stone. The pointed windows and the chapel vaulting in the forebuilding are among the earliest known examples of Gothic architecture in England.

English Heritage. Open throughout the year.

SURREY

Farnham

Between 1129 and 1171 Henry of Blois, Bishop of Winchester, built a castle on the road from Winchester to London. The first keep was a square tower on a 30 foot (9 m) mound and two of the wooden piers are still preserved in the great hall. During the thirteenth century a chapel was added and stone replaced wood. William of Wykeham enlarged the bishop's quarters and Bishop Waynflete added the brick entry tower. It must have been impressive because both Henry VII and Henry VIII stayed at Farnham.

In the seventeenth century James I used Farnham as a hunting seat. It was strengthened by Parliament during the Civil War, but after Edgehill, the commander, George Wither, abandoned it to the Royalists. Charles placed Sir John Denham there with a small force but this was not strong enough to hold out against Sir William Waller in December 1642 and for a time it was used as a prison for captured Royalists; in 1648 it was slighted. Alterations and improvements were made in the eighteenth and nineteenth centuries and from 1927 to 1955 it belonged to the Bishops of Guildford.

In 1958 excavations revealed the base of the square keep and a deep well shaft. The visitor today can examine the foundations and see the original ground level. The tower must have been about 70 feet (21 m) high.

English Heritage. Keep only open, April to September.

SURREY

Guildford

The fine Norman keep of Guildford's castle, once used as a jail, stands in a public garden off Quarry Street, dating from Henry II's reign although the surrounding walls are older. The castle was a favourite royal residence in the thirteenth century. *Garden open at all times. Keep open regularly from Easter to September.*

TYNE AND WEAR

Newcastle

The Romans first fortified the Tyne at Newcastle, where Hadrian built the first bridge. The Normans had a fort here and then Henry II constructed the new castle in 1172-7, but now only the keep, the Black Gate and a part of the curtain remain.

The Black Gate was built in 1247 and houses the Bagpipe Museum. It consists of a vaulted passage and twin towers. It was the main entrance of the castle leading to a drawbridge across a ditch and the North Gate.

The massive keep, dating from 1172, has walls 15 feet (4.6 m) thick and an entrance through a forebuilding to the second floor. During the Civil War the Scots captured Newcastle but the mayor and Sir John Marley held out for a further three days in the keep. After that it was used for many years as a jail. It has a hall and king's chamber, and battlements restored in 1809 by William Dobson. The chapel is below the hall and has a fine zigzag frieze.

Newcastle upon Tyne City Council. Open throughout the year.

Tynemouth

In the grounds of the Priory at Tynemouth, Robert de Mowbray built a wall and ditch with a strong gatehouse. Licence to crenellate dates from 1296 and the gatehouse dates from the early fifteenth century. It had bartisan towers and was protected by a barbican.

English Heritage. Unrestricted access.

WARWICKSHIRE

Kenilworth

The only lake fortress in England, Kenilworth was granted to Geoffrey de Clinton by Henry I. The first building was probably a motte and bailey castle but the first stone structure was the massive twelfth-century keep, which was built by Geoffrey's son. Between 1212 and 1216 Kenilworth was the property of King John. Lunn's Tower and Water Tower were constructed at the king's expense and many other improvements were carried out.

Henry III's sister Eleanor married Simon de Montfort, Earl of Leicester, and the castle was granted first to Eleanor and in 1254 to them both for life. With its wide meres and moat Kenilworth made an ideal centre for de Montfort's rebellion. In 1264, Simon sent Henry's brother Richard and his youngest son Edmund to Kenilworth as prisoners, the king and Prince Edward being held at Hereford. The following year Prince Edward escaped and attacked Simon's son, who was camping with his soldiers outside the castle. Young Simon was nearly captured but escaped into the castle, which, following the elder Simon's defeat at Evesham, was besieged for six months. The defenders dressed up one of their men as a priest to excommunicate the attackers, but finally disease and hunger forced the surrender and young Simon fled abroad.

During the Civil War the castle was used as quarters for Parliamentary troops but the owner, Lord Monmouth, was unable to prevent the unnecessary slighting that took place in 1649, when the keep was destroyed and huge gaps were made in the outer walls. Colonel Hawksworth, who carried out the demolition work, then occupied the habitable part with ten other officers. He drained the mere and ignored decaying stonework.

Charles II granted Kenilworth to Laurence Hyde, whose son became the Earl of Clarendon. It remained in their family until 1958 when it was presented to the people of Kenilworth and came under the guardianship of the Ministry of Public Building and Works.

English Heritage. Open throughout the year.

Maxstoke

One of the most perfectly preserved private castles of the fourteenth century, Maxstoke stands in extensive grounds near Coleshill.

The licence to crenellate Maxstoke was granted by Edward III to William de Clinton, Earl of Huntingdon, in 1346. From the Clintons it passed in 1438 to Humphrey, Earl of Stafford. The four octagonal towers guarded the curtain wall, which is surrounded by a moat, and the entrance has iron and wooden doors. Maxstoke was more a residential castle than a military one. Richard III is supposed to have spent a night before Bosworth at Maxstoke. Sir Thomas Egerton, Lord Keeper of the Great Seal, subsequently lived there. Edward Stafford, Lord High Constable of England, lived here during Henry VIII's reign but, through Wolsey's influence, fell out of favour and was beheaded in 1521, whereupon the castle passed to Sir William Compton. It was later purchased by the Dilkes of Kirkby Mallory, whose descendants still live there.

Captain C. B. Fetherston-Dilke, RN. Open to organised parties by written appointment only. Garden open under the National Gardens Scheme one day a year.

Warwick

William the Conqueror ordered a new and enlarged castle to be built here on the site of Saxon fortifications. Henry de Newburgh was made its constable and was later created Earl of Warwick.

The castle remained Crown property and the Earl was merely the custodian. During the Barons' War the Earl was forcibly removed to Kenilworth by John Gifford and held to ransom. In 1265 he died and the title passed through his daughter to the Beauchamp family.

The two successive Thomas Beauchamps, Earls of Warwick, were responsible for building most of the castle that stands today. Both Guy's and Caesar's towers were constructed at this time. Guy's Tower is twelve-sided and rises to 128 feet (39 m); Caesar's Tower resembles three towers squashed together with an inner stage and rises to 147 feet (45 m). In 1356 French prisoners captured at Poitiers were accommodated in Guy's Tower.

The famous Richard Neville, Earl of Warwick, inherited the castle from the Beauchamps and it remained in Yorkist hands. After Warwick's death at the battle of Barnet in 1471 the title of Earl of Warwick went to the unfortunate Clarence, his son-in-law, who met his death by drowning in wine. The unfinished Bear and Clarence towers are the remains of the artillery fort started, but never finished, by Richard III, and which originally consisted of four towers. The Bear Tower contains a pit which is thought to have been a bear pit. Richard III's nephew Edward was beheaded by Henry VII on a trumped-up charge, and for sixty years there was no Earl of Warwick. Henry VIII bestowed the earldom on John Dudley, a relation of the Beauchamps, and it was this Earl, later made Duke of Northumberland, who tried to put his daughter-in-law Lady Jane Grey on the throne and lost his life in the attempt. His son Ambrose inherited the title and when he died childless in 1589 it reverted to the Crown. James I bestowed the title, but not the castle, on Lord Rich of Leigh.

In 1604 Fulke Greville had obtained a grant of the castle and had repaired it at great expense until it became 'the most princely seat within the midland parts of this realm'. Fulke, a man of letters and a courtier, was stabbed by his servant in 1628 and his cousin Robert, Lord Brooke, inherited the castle. Robert was a Parliamentary supporter and took part in the battle of Edgehill. For three days Warwick was besieged by the Royalists under Lord Northampton. Sir Edward Peto, in charge of the garrison, refused to surrender. Robert was killed at Lichfield. His successor was a Royalist, who was responsible for the fitting up of the present magnificent state apartments.
Madame Tussaud's. Open daily, except Christmas Day.

WEST MIDLANDS

Dudley

Dudley Castle was probably built by William Fitzansculf, who held it at the time of Domesday. Later it passed to the Paganels and when in 1173 Gervase de Paganel joined the revolt against Henry II, the latter dismantled it. The castle, part of which we see today, was built in about 1270 by John de Somery. In 1322 the castle passed to John de Somery's brother-in-law. Captured at St Albans in 1445, he was imprisoned in the Tower and after the accession of Edward IV changed sides. During the reign of Henry VII, Lord Dudley, his descendant, known as Lord Quondam, sold the castle to his cousin John Dudley, Duke of Northumberland. In 1554 Northumberland was executed for high treason for trying to put his daughter-in-law, Lady Jane Grey, on the throne. Dudley Castle was then returned to Edward Sutton, the son of John Sutton, who had lost it to Northumberland. During the Civil War Dudley was garrisoned for the King and held out until 1646 when Colonel Leveson surrendered. In 1647 Parliament ordered the slighting of the castle. On 24th July 1750 a fire, which burned until the 26th, began in the living quarters and completely gutted them.
Dudley Castle and Zoo. Open throughout the year.

Weoley

Off Alwold Road, Selly Oak, Birmingham archaeologists have excavated the six-towered castle built in the thirteenth century by Roger de Somery and his son John. Later owned by the Berkeleys until 1485, it was allowed to decay when it passed to the Jervoise family. There is a small museum.
Birmingham Museums. Open March to October.

WEST SUSSEX

Amberley

The castle lies south of Pulborough on B2139 and was a twelfth century manor house belonging to the Bishops of Chichester. In 1377 Bishop Rede obtained a licence to crenellate from Richard II and built the high walls that stand today and added a great hall, connected by the solar to the main house. A water gate was constructed in the west wall. There does not appear to have been a moat on this side. Bishop Sherburne restored the Queen's Room above the dining hall in about 1530 and nine panels of classical scenes were painted by Lambert Bernard at this time.
Mr Hollis M. Baker. Not open to the public.

Arundel

The Duke of Norfolk's large castle comprises a large motte and two baileys dating from 1067, an eleventh-century gatehouse, twelfth-century shell-keep and thirteenth-century barbican. The residential part, however, is mostly a Victorian restoration in Gothic style, and its history and contents are of more interest than its architecture, although from the south, especially, it presents a magnificent spectacle.

Earl Roger de Montgomery was originally granted the Rape of Arundel after the Battle of Hastings and he founded the castle. Robert de Belleme, who inherited Arundel from Earl Roger, sided with the Duke of Normandy against Henry I.

The castle came into the possession of the Albini family, the last of whom died in 1243, and Arundel passed to his daughter Isabel, who married John Fitzalan, son of the lord of Clun Castle. The Fitzalans lived here until 1580 when the last, Henry, Earl of Arundel, died. His daughter succeeded to the property with her husband, Thomas Howard, Duke of Norfolk. It has remained Norfolk property ever since. During the Civil War the third and longest siege took place. The constable, Sir Edward Ford, held out bravely for eighteen days but on 6th January 1644 he surrendered to Sir William Waller after the walls had been battered by cannon placed in the tower of St Nicholas's church.

Arundel remained a ruin until the eighth Duke began restoring it in 1716 and this work was continued by the eleventh Duke in 1789. One of the rooms added was the library with its mahogany woodwork, which was completed in 1801. The fifteenth Duke finalised restoration work from 1875 to 1903 to the design of C. A. Buckler. A total of £600,000 was spent on its restoration.

The Duke of Norfolk. Open regularly April to October.

Bramber

William de Braose built a castle here, of which there remains only a tall wall of one side of the keep. It was garrisoned by Captain Temple in 1644 and blown up when captured by the Parliamentarians. At one time ships came up the Adur and there were salt pans beneath the walls and a moat on the south and north-west sides.

National Trust. Open at all times.

WEST YORKSHIRE

Pontefract

One of the most famous of English castles, Pontefract was constructed on the route between Doncaster and York. It was begun by Ilbert de Lacy in the late eleventh century. Henry de Lacy, Earl of Lincoln, lived here in the mid thirteenth century.

After his two sons died — one fell from a tower and the other was drowned in Denbigh — the castle passed by marriage to Thomas, Earl of Lancaster, who led the rising that ended ignominiously at Boroughbridge. After being confined here he was beheaded on St Thomas's Hill. Like Pickering, the castle then passed to John of Gaunt and later to Henry Bolingbroke. Richard II ended his days here after submitting to Henry at Flint.

As a prison, Pontefract held James I of Scotland and also the Duke of Orleans and other French prisoners from Agincourt. It was a key Lancastrian stronghold in the Wars of the Roses, at the battle of Wakefield and on Edward IV's return. When Richard of Gloucester made his bid for the throne, Sir Thomas Vaughan was imprisoned here and later beheaded here together with Lord Grey and Earl Rivers. In 1536 the Pilgrimage of Grace captured Pontefract from Lord Darcy, who later supported the cause.

During the Civil War it was besieged by Fairfax from December 1644 and relieved by Sir Marmaduke Longdale's Northern Horse in March 1645. It was captured for Parliament in the second siege, of July 1645, by General Poyntz. In 1648 the castle was recaptured by Royalist forces when they drove carts carrying concealed soldiers into the bailey. After a siege lasting a year the Royalist garrison surrendered in 1649 after provisions had been exhausted and the execution of the King had ended their cause. Following the surrender the slighting of the castle was so thorough that little now remains. Part of the Swillington Tower can still be seen by the road while a few low walls is all that remains of the great tower. The revetments down the motte of the great tower have also been excavated. The entrance is at the end of Micklegate.

Open throughout the year. Museum.

Sandal Magna

The ruins of Sandal Castle, just outside Wakefield, are on the hill near the church. The original building dates from about 1157 but the stone structure was not built until about 1320 by Earl Warenne. During the Wars of the Roses Richard, Duke of York, owned Sandal and he was killed when he left its safety during the battle of Wakefield in 1460. The Earl of Wiltshire captured Sandal and over two thousand Yorkists were killed. It was the most overwhelming Lancastrian victory of the war. Richard III came here from time to time and later it belonged to the Saviles of Thornhill. During the Civil War it was held for the king by Colonel Bonivant and surrendered in October 1645. It was slighted the following year. Much recent excavation work has been carried out by the Wakefield Historical Society and

their excellent booklets provide a fascinating picture of the castle's construction.
Wakefield Corporation. Open to the public at all times.

WILTSHIRE

Ludgershall

Extensive earthworks remain today, including the site of the Great Hall, built for Henry III's son. Excavations have found that there were other buildings here and that Ludgershall was once an important royal residence.
English Heritage. Open at all times.

Old Sarum

In 1070 the Conqueror reviewed his victorious army in Old Sarum, and it was at this time that the great circular earthwork was constructed in the centre of a magnificent iron age fort. The outer fortifications were increased to their present dimensions. The cathedral church, whose remains can still be seen, was consecrated in 1092 and improved by Bishop Roger of Salisbury between 1107 and 1139. By 1447 the castle was in decay and the town was abandoned in the fifteenth century.
English Heritage. Open throughout the year.

Old Wardour

The fourteenth-century castle, shaped like a keyhole with the main entrance facing east, was built by John, Lord Lovell, who obtained a licence to crenellate in 1393. The daughter of Lord Lovell married Lord Dynham and their granddaughter married an Arundel. Sir Matthew Arundel's coat of arms and the date 1570 are above the door and his successor Sir Thomas, the first Lord Arundel, distinguished himself fighting against the Turks in 1595. The second Lord Arundel raised a troop to fight for Charles I and left his wife, Blanche, the daughter of the Marquess of Worcester, at Wardour with a small garrison. In May 1643 Colonel Strode attacked it with thirteen hundred men and for five days the garrison held out. Two mines under the fabric did little damage but Lady Blanche decided to surrender as food and ammunition supplies were short. Colonel Ludlow now put in a Parliamentary garrison. After the death of the second lord at Lansdowne, the third lord raised a small army to regain his castle. In March 1644 he succeeded after blowing up the corn store and killing three of the garrison. The colonel surrendered and the Arundels returned to live in an outhouse, for the main structure had been too badly damaged to be habitable. The eighth lord built the new castle nearby, between 1769 and 1776. This is now a girls' school.
English Heritage. Open throughout the year.

Castles of Wales

CLWYD

Chirk

On A5 between Shrewsbury and Llangollen, Chirk Castle stands on the Welsh border in the middle of a large estate. During the war between Llywelyn the Last and Edward I Roger Mortimer played a notable part. As a reward he was granted the lands of Chirk, where there was a castle near the church. He built a new castle between 1274 and 1310, probably incorporating some of the old castle material at Chirk. This was rectangular in plan with a circular tower in each corner and parapets wide enough for two men to walk abreast. There were two other castles on the same land, Castel y Waun and Dinas Bran, both at Llangollen, which had been built by Gruffydd ap Madoc.

Chirk passed from the Mortimers to the Arundels and the Mowbrays. In 1397 Mowbray was executed for treason and the estate passed to the Beauchamps. Edward IV presented it to Lord Stanley, famous for his late intervention at Bosworth. He was executed in 1495 for supporting Perkin Warbeck, so Chirk passed to the King. Henry VIII gave it to Thomas Seymour and Elizabeth I granted it to her favourite, the Earl of Leicester. It was sold to Sir Thomas Myddelton in 1595 and it remains the home of the Myddelton family today.

His son, another Sir Thomas, was MP for Denbighshire and during the Civil War was made Major-General of the Parliamentary forces in North Wales. During his absence Colonel Ellis captured Chirk for the Royalists and Colonel Watts was made governor. In 1644 Myddelton besieged Chirk, but as it was his own home he did not want to use artillery. With planks and tables he tried to get in through a drain but Watts rained stones down on him and killed his engineer. In 1646 Sir John Watts (he had been knighted by Charles I), realising the war was over, surrendered Chirk and the garrison 'stole all privately away'.

In 1659 Myddelton, restored to his lands, supported the cause of Charles II. He was a year too early and General Lambert attacked Chirk with cannon, causing considerable damage. At the Restoration he was awarded the large sum of £30,000 for its repair. during the next few years the long gallery was constructed and many of the present treasures were purchased for the castle. The dining room decoration dates from the eighteenth century and much work was done by Pugin in the nineteenth century, but Chirk remains unspoilt as one of the few inhabited castles in Wales.

Lieutenant Colonel R. Myddelton. Open regularly April to October.

Denbigh

One of the most ruinous and yet most interesting of all the Welsh castles, Denbigh stands high up in the centre of the town. Dafydd ap Gruffydd, Llywelyn's brother, lived here for a time. The castle, built by Hugh de Lacy, Earl of Lincoln, in 1282 was probably built on the site of Dafydd's fortified house. The Welsh captured Denbigh in the revolt of 1294 but de Lacy recaptured it, dying before it was completed in 1311. The castle passed to Thomas, Earl of Lancaster, de Lacy's son-in-law, who was executed in 1322 at Pontefract, after his defeat at Borough-bridge. Edward II granted it to his favourite Hugh Despenser but after he was hanged at Bristol the property passed to Roger Mortimer, who suffered the same fate at Tyburn in 1330.

After this the castle passed through several hands until it became the headquarters of Henry Percy (Hotspur) in 1399. During the Wars of the Roses it changed hands more than once. Japser Tudor burnt it in 1468 when it was held by the Yorkists and henceforth the town was constructed outside the old town walls — the gate on the north-west side still stands — with the exception of Leicester's Chapel which lies below the castle and appears never to have been completed.

Robert Dudley, Earl of Leicester, owned Denbigh from 1563 to 1588, when it reverted to the crown. During the Civil War it was garrisoned for the King by Colonel Salesbury and Charles came here after his defeat at Rowton Heath. The castle was besieged from April to 26th October 1646, when, on the command of the king, Salesbury surrendered to General Mytton. The Royalists marched out 'with flying colours, drums beating, matches lit at both ends, bullets in the mouth and every soldier with twelve charges of powder'. The castle was destroyed just before the Restoration so today only a portion of the gatehouse with its three towers, some ruinous walls and bases of other towers remain.

Inside the gatehouse to the right is a small museum.
Cadw. Open throughout the year.

Dinas Bran

One of the most spectacular castles in Wales, Dinas Bran looks down from its heights above Llangollen. Once the home of Madoc ap Gruffydd Maelor, founder of Valle Crucis Abbey, in 1390 it was the home of Myfanwy Fechan. By 1578 it was already being described as a ruin. To reach it, take the road over the river from the A5 and carry on over the canal past the Catholic church.
Ruins open at all times.

Ewloe

One of the surprising castles of North Wales, Ewloe is easy to miss. It lies a few miles out of Hawarden on A55 to Holywell and is not visible from the road. It was built about 1146 when Mold Castle was captured by Owain Gwynedd. Near here Owain won a battle against Henry II.

The Welsh Tower with its south external staircase dates from about 1200 and the lower ward and west tower were probably built by Llywelyn. In 1277 the building of Flint Castle and the conquest of the area by Edward I lessened the importance of Ewloe. The castle has a well in the lower ward but there is no trace of a chapel but it could have been in the south-east tower which no longer remains. In 1922 the ruins were covered in ivy and the Ministry cleaned out fallen stones and earth, building up the floor of the north side and making the approach to the ruin easier.

Cadw. Open April to September.

Flint

The first of Edward I's great castles stands on the Dee estuary in the middle of an industrial area. It was originally supplied from the sea and had a moat round the outer bailey. The great tower was unusually placed outside the main curtain and is connected by a separate drawbridge. Inside the keep has a circular gallery with three doors and steps down to the central chamber. The tower was fitted with a wooden brattice so archers could command the drawbridge. Flint was not completed until 1280 and was besieged in 1282 by Llywelyn, whose death that year ended the war.

In August 1399 Richard II was at Flint when Henry Bolingbroke forced him to abdicate. During the Civil War Flint changed hands on more than one occasion. It was garrisoned by Roger Mostyn, a young Royalist Colonel, and in 1646 it was closely besieged by Brereton's Parliamentary army, fresh from the capture of Caernarfon. Mostyn let his cavalry escape and resisted until his provisions ran out, when he surrendered on honourable terms. In 1652 the castle was slighted.

Cadw. Open throughout the year.

Hawarden

On old road from Chester to Conwy and Bangor, Hawarden Castle dates from the reign of Edward I and was built by the Montalts to keep the Welsh at bay. During the Barons' War Simon de Montfort's son Henry met Llywelyn here and granted him the castle. The English failed to keep their word, and in 1265 the Welsh prince and his army destroyed it. Montalt was captured and forced to swear not to fortify the castle again. He was released in 1267 and the castle was rebuilt about ten years later. Once again in 1282 the Welsh attacked and captured it, Roger Clifford, the constable, being taken prisoner in his bed. It was rebuilt by Edward I.

During the Civil War Hawarden remained, for the most part, in Royalist hands. The Parliamentarians captured it briefly in 1643 but were flung out by an Irish force commanded by Sir Michael Ernley and Captain Sandford. Sir William Neale then garrisoned the castle until 16th March 1646, when he surrendered after obtaining permission from the king.

The keep and large sections of the curtain wall survive. The new building to the east, originally Hawarden House, constructed in 1752 and gothicised early in the nineteenth century, became famous as the home of W. E. Gladstone.

Open Sunday afternoons, Easter to August. Part of the park is open at all reasonable times.

Rhuddlan

Rhuddlan has long been important as it commands the ford over the river Clwyd, protecting the road from Chester to Conwy.

Edward I chose Rhuddlan as his base for the conquest of Wales, starting to build here after Flint and continuing after the surrender of Llywelyn in 1282. A new site was chosen and, under the capable control of James of St George, Rhuddlan was constructed so that it could be supplied from the sea. A dyke was built and the river diverted. Men were brought in from all over England to dig the ditch and moat and some kind of swing-bridge was constructed so that ships of up to 40 tons could sail right up to the castle. The castle originally had three gates, the Turret Gate at the south-east, the River Gate on the west, and the Town Gate, which had a complicated turning bridge and stood at the end of the moat. It appears the bridge never spanned the moat as there is a pit where the bridge must have been. Edward used the castle for his wars in 1277 and 1282 and in 1284 he promised to present the Welsh people with a 'Prince born in Wales, who could speak no English and whose life and conversation nobody could stain.' Young Edward, later Edward II, who was born at Caernarfon, was the first Prince of Wales but history has not recorded where the ceremony took place.

Rhuddlan was drastically slighted during the Civil War after Colonel Mytton had captured the castle for Parliament. The towers give the impression of having been fired on from close range as only their base portions are substantially damaged.

Rhuddlan has, unlike the other Edwardian castles, two main entrances to the diamond-shaped inner ward.

Cadw. Open throughout the year.

Ruthin

The first reference to Ruthin Castle, which is now a large, mostly Victorian, hotel, was in 1282, when it was taken by Reginald de Grey in the war against Llywelyn and used as his headquarters. De Grey, one of Edward I's generals, had a force of about four hundred infantry under his command until the death of Llywelyn in Builth at the end of 1282. In 1294 when Caernarfon was seized in another Welsh rising, de Grey raised five thousand men and saved Flint, Rhuddlan and the land east of Ruthin from capture and destruction.

The castle was enlarged and mostly rebuilt by de Grey. Originally a small Welsh stronghold, it was turned into a large seven-towered rectangular castle, the north side being angled outwards where the main entrance gate was covered by the central and eastern towers. The third baron, another Reginald de Grey, quarrelled with Owain Glyndwr, who attacked Ruthin in September 1400, burning the town but failing to capture the castle. Two years later de Grey was captured when outside his castle walls by Glyndwr's men, who held him hostage in Snowdonia until the large ransom of about £650,000 was paid. This payment ruined the de Greys and in 1508 the castle was sold to the Crown.

At the beginning of the Civil War Ruthin belonged to Sir Thomas Myddelton, the owner of Chirk. This was a Royalist area, however, and Ruthin was garrisoned for the king. Myddelton failed to capture it and later it held out for three months against General Mytton. Traditionally supplies were brought in through an underground passage from the Red Lion in Clwyd Street. The governor, Colonel Trevor, finally surrendered on favourable terms and in 1647 the inevitable slighting took place.

The present building was erected by the Myddelton-Wests in 1849 and was designed by Henry Clutton. The last descendant of the Myddeltons was Theresa, whose guardian was Admiral Cornwallis. She married Frederick West and they were known as Cornwallis-West. In the hotel today the portrait of Mary Cornwallis-West by Gordigiani is a pleasant reminder of the last links with the seventeenth-century owner.

Guide books and postcards available at the hotel. The castle is not open to visitors.

DYFED

Aberystwyth

Near St Michael's church, the ruins of Aberystwyth Castle overlook the sea and have been formed into a small park. The castle was built by Edmund Crouchback, brother of Edward I, and was concentric in plan, the outer walls measuring 160 yards (146 m) from north to south and 80 yards (73 m) from east to west. It fell to Owain Glyndwr in 1404 and was recaptured by Prince Henry in 1408.

During the Civil War it was held by the Royalists until attacked and captured by Parliamentary forces in 1646. The governor was Colonel Roger Whitley, who was second in command of the Royalists in Anglesey. Although captured in Beaumaris, he lived to see not only the Restoration but the accession of William III, when he became a Whig and was made Mayor of Chester.

Open at all times.

Carew

Just off the main A477 between Pembroke and Kilgetty, Carew has one of the most interesting and compact castles in Wales. The earliest building, a motte and bailey, was constructed by Gerald de Windsor in 1105. He acquired the property in 1100 as part of the dowry of his wife, Nesta, daughter of Rhys ap Tewdwr, King of Deheubarth. Their son William took the name de Carew, and another de Carew, Nicholas, built the three Norman towers, the massive west front and the chapel in the late thirteenth century. He died in 1311. The gatehouse, porch and steps to the great hall were added by Sir Rhys ap Thomas, who leased the castle from Sir Edmund Carew in 1480. Sir Rhys welcomed Henry Tudor when he landed at Dale in 1485 and marched with him to Bosworth Field. Sir Rhys held a great tournament here in 1507 and over six hundred nobles with their attendants were present. Sir Rhys died in 1525. Queen Mary granted Carew to Sir John Perrot, the Lord Deputy of Ireland, in 1557. Sir John was believed to be the natural son of Henry VIII and looked much like him. He hoped to entertain Elizabeth I at Carew and built the lavish north wing with its two oriels and magnificent mullioned windows. The building was never finished as Sir John was accused of treason and imprisoned in the Tower of London, where he died in 1592.

The Castle reverted to the Carew family in 1601 and declared for the King in the Civil War. It fell to Parliamentary forces in 1645; considerable damage was done to the south wall and the Kitchen Tower was demolished.

There is a grisly legend associated with Sir Roland Rhys, who is said to have lived in the castle during the reign of James I. His son married the daughter of a Flemish tradesman named Horwitz, who was a tenant of Sir Roland, against his father's wishes. One stormy night Horwitz called to pay his rent. Sir Roland in a moment of anger set his pet ape on Horwitz but he escaped and was sheltered by Sir Roland's servant. There were fearful screams in the middle of the night and it was discovered that the ape had killed its master and pulled the fire out of the hearth, burning itself to death and setting fire to the room. Henceforth the withdrawing room adjoining the great hall, was said to be haunted by Sir Roland's ghost.

The present owner, a direct descendant of Gerald and Nesta, has leased the castle to the Pembrokeshire Coast National Park Authority, and has commenced on conserving this historic building.

Mr Anthony Trollope-Bellew. Open Easter to October.

Carreg Cennen

The spectacular castle of the Cennen valley, some 7 miles (11 km) south-east of Llandeilo, was built in the thirteenth century on the site of a Roman fort. In 1254 it was taken by Rhys Fychan, one of the sons of Lord Rhys. In 1282 Lord Rhys's wife took the castle from her son and delivered it to the English, but it was recaptured by Gruffydd and Llywelyn, sons of Rhys Fychan. They could not hold if for long, however, and in 1283 it passed to John Giffard, owner of Llandovery Castle.

In 1323 Edward II granted it to his favourite Hugh Despencer after Giffard had been executed for treason. It changed ownership on Hugh's downfall and eventually passed in 1362 to John of Gaunt and the Duchy of Lancaster. In 1403, when the defences must have been complete, it held out against Owain Glyndwr under its constable, John Skydmore. During the Wars of the Roses it was held by Gruffydd ap Nicholas, whose sons fought for the Lancastrian army at Mortimer's Cross in 1461. The following year a Yorkist force commanded by Sir Richard Herbert of Raglan and Sir Roger Vaughan of Tretower captured Carreg Cennen and, because it had become the headquarters of thieves, it was demolished by the Sheriff of Carmarthenshire for £28 5s 6d. In the nineteenth century the ruins were restored by the Earl of Cawdor.

The approaches to the castle are unusually complicated. There were two gates with drawbridges over deep pits and a square prison tower commanding the final approach. There is a mysterious cave in the south-east corner of the Inner Ward. It is approached by a long narrow passage and may have once led out to the Outer Ward.

Cadw. Open throughout the year.

Cilgerran

Cilgerran on the Teifi is 2 miles (3 km) south of Cardigan. It was built by the Norman Gerald of Windsor in about 1110 and captured and recaptured by the Welsh and English until the present castle was built about 1233.

In the fourteenth century Cilgerran belonged to the Hastings family, but in 1326 it had fallen into ruins. In 1377 Edward III ordered that Cilgerran, as well as Tenby and Pembroke castles, should be repaired in case of French invasion and the square north-west tower was added. In 1405 it fell to Owain Glyndwr and in 1414 it passed to the Duke of Gloucester, brother of Henry V. After Henry VII's accession it was granted to the Vaughan family, who lived here until the building of their new house nearby in the seventeenth century.

Cilgerran is unusual in two respects. It has no keep and no wall. The east and west towers in the inner curtain served in place of a keep and the postern gate gave access to the river for water, but in a siege this must have been dangerous as the path is exposed to the opposite bank. Excavation has uncovered the old gatehouse to the outer ward. The castle has been well restored. *Cadw. Open throughout the year.*

Dinefwr

Modern Dinefwr Castle, near Llandeilo, was built in 1856. The old castle is thirteenth-century. In 876 the site was held by Rhodri Mawr against the Danes. In Norman times it held out against the conquest under its constable, Rhys ap Tewdwr, but was eventually captured and rebuilt. In 1257 it was besieged by the English and Llywelyn raised the siege. Henry VIII seized it from Sir Rhys ap Thomas on a trumped-up charge of treason and executed him. In the eighteenth century it was damaged by fire and today only the round keep and a square tower with a moat carved out of the rock are visible over the river Towy. *Cadw. Opening to the public in the 1990s.*

Dryslwyn

A few miles from Dinefwr, on top of a steep hill, the castle belonged to Lord Rhys ap Meredudd, who rebelled against the English in 1287 and captured Swansea. The Earl of Cornwall attacked him at Dryslwyn with eleven thousand men and undermined the castle. William de Montchensh and about 150 Staffordshire men were killed when the mine caved in and part of the castle collapsed. Eventually captured at York, Rhys was tried and executed, his castle going to Robert of Tibetot. *Open at all times. The castle can be reached up a farm track off B4297.*

Haverfordwest

Like Pembroke, the castle at Haverfordwest completely dominates the town. It was constructed about 1120 by Gilbert de Clare and after being virtually demolished was considerably strengthened by William de Valence in the thirteenth century. In

1405 it withstood an attack by over two thousand men who landed at Milford Haven from France to support Owain Glyndwr. During the Civil War it surrendered to Parliament and after the Second Civil War in 1648 the inner ward was blown up and in the eighteenth century was made into a prison. In the record office there are two plans of the French landing in 1797 at Carreg Wastad. Haverfordwest sent its militia out to round up the French and two Welshmen, suspected of fraternising with the enemy, were thrown into the castle jail.

The castle has been converted into a museum and art gallery and also houses the Pembrokeshire Record Office. The museum contains a special display on the Norman conquest of Wales and the development of the castle, with a model of old Haverfordwest.

Dyfed County Council. Open throughout the year.

Kidwelly

Kidwelly lies on A484 between Carmarthen and Llanelli. The castle and town stand at the head of the wide estuary of the river Gwendraeth overlooking a flat expanse of marsh. The first castle was erected by Roger, Bishop of Salisbury, in 1115. In 1136 a battle was fought between Gwenllian, wife of Gruffydd ap Rhys, and Maurice de Londres, constable of the castle. The Welsh were defeated and Gwenllian and her son killed.

Kidwelly was once a fortified town and a fourteenth-century gateway remains in Bailey Street. The river protected the eastern flank and a deep ditch the western flank. There is a small motte in front of the main gatehouse which might be the motte of the original castle. The inner ward dates from the thirteenth century and the hall, chapel and living quarters were possibly constructed during the minority of Matilda de Chaworth. The gatehouse was only completed about 1400, and in 1402 the Welsh, aided by a French force, damaged the roof and finally a new hall was constructed in the outer ward.

During the fifteenth century it belonged to the Tudors and in the sixteenth to the Earls of Cawdor, one of whom presented it to the Ministry of Works in 1927.

Cadw. Open throughout the year.

Laugharne

Between Llanstephan and Pendine, the keep and Henry II tower still remain of the thirteenth-century castle. At the beginning of the fourteenth century it was held by Sir Guy de Brian. Sir John Perrot rebuilt it as his home during the sixteenth century and it was captured by Parliament during the Civil War.

Open at all reasonable times. Apply to Castle House by the Town Hall.

Llandovery

On A40 between Brecon and Llandeilo, Llandovery Castle is a motte with a ruined shell-keep in the car park. The first record of the castle is in 1116 when, attacked by the Welsh, it was held by Richard de Pons. In 1208 it was captured for a short time by Rhys Fychan. The English strengthened it and once more the Welsh under Rhys ap Meredudd captured it. Edward I made peace with Rhys, who was traditionally an enemy of Llywelyn, and thereafter Llandovery remained in English hands. It appears to have played no further part until its ultimate destruction by Cromwell.

Unrestricted access.

Llanstephan

Opposite Kidwelly on the Towy estuary, Llanstephan Castle was built on an iron age site, probably by Gilbert de Clare. It was captured by the Welsh princes in 1146. Young Prince Maredudd flung down the Norman scaling ladders when an attempt was made to recapture it. Henry II took it and gave it to William de Camville, who strengthened it in 1192. Another William de Camville died in 1338 and the castle went to his daughter and her husband, Robert de Penrees. In 1403 it was captured by Owain Glyndwr and held for three months. In 1443 it passed to the Crown. Henry VII presented it to his uncle Jasper Tudor in 1495. In the eighteenth century it reverted to private hands. *Cadw. Open at all reasonable times.*

Llawhaden

A few miles north of Narberth, near the junction of A40 and A476, Llawhaden Castle was built in the early twelfth century to protect the property of the Bishop of St Davids who had his house surrounded by a palisade and a moat. Destroyed by Lord Rhys in 1193, it was rebuilt by Thomas Bek in 1280 as a fortified mansion. Of the circular pattern of the earlier building only the tower base on the west bank now remains. A large hall and kitchens with two very deep wells were completed in the fourteenth century by Bishop Martyn. Later the gatehouse on the south-west side was improved.

During the early sixteenth century Bishop Morgan seized a Lady Tanglost and accused her of witchcraft. She was imprisoned at Llawhaden, but her friend Thomas Wyriott attacked the castle with his retainers and rescued her, though she was later imprisoned again. Shortly after this the lead was removed from the castle roof in an attempt to enforce the removal of the see of St David's to Carmarthen. Llawhaden thus became a ruin. *Cadw. Open throughout the year.*

30. Ludlow Castle, Shropshire.

31. Stokesay Castle, Shropshire.

32. *Upton Cressett Hall, Shropshire.*

33. *Conisbrough Castle, South Yorkshire.*

34. Farleigh Hungerford Castle, Somerset.

35. Nunney Castle, Somerset.

36. Tamworth Castle, Staffordshire.
37. Bungay Castle, Suffolk.

38. *Framlingham Castle, Suffolk.*

39. *Kenilworth Castle, Warwickshire.*

40. *Warwick Castle, Warwickshire.*

41. *Bramber Castle, West Sussex.*

42. *Arundel Castle, West Sussex.*

43. *Clifford's Tower, York, North Yorkshire.*

44. *Flint Castle, Clwyd.*

45. Rhuddlan Castle, Clwyd.

46. *Carew Castle, Dyfed.*

47. *Manorbier Castle, Dyfed.*

48. Roch Castle, Dyfed.

49. Pembroke Castle, Dyfed.

50. Chepstow Castle, Gwent.

51. White Castle, Gwent.

52. Raglan Castle, Gwent.

53. *Beaumaris Castle, Gwynedd.*

54. *Conwy Castle, Gwynedd.*

55. *Coity Castle, Mid Glamorgan.*

56. *Cardiff Castle, South Glamorgan.*

Manorbier

3 miles (5 km) from Pembroke on the south coast is the famous castle of Odo de Barri dating from the twelfth century. Its name is derived from the Welsh word *maenor* and Pyr, a sixth-century abbot of Caldy Island. Odo's famous grandson, Geraldus Cambrensis, was born here about 1146. His father William de Barri sent him to Paris, where he became a scholar at the university and visited Rome. He wrote his famous itinerary in which he describes in detail twelfth-century life in Wales. Manorbier is, he says, 'conspicuous by its towers and ramparts', possessing fine fishponds and 'a most excellent harbour for shipping'. Gerald's main ambition was to make the Welsh church independent by creating an archbishopric at St Davids, and it was this unsuccessful, ecclesiastical struggle with Henry II which made him famous in his own day. The castle passed from the de Barris in the fourteenth century and then through various hands until Elizabeth I sold it to Thomas ap Owen of Treflayne. It came by marriage into the Philipps family of Picton Castle.

The structure that stands today is the inner ward with the remains of the state apartments at the south-west and a private residence, which was added in the nineteenth century and stands next to the twelfth-century round tower. The only siege it suffered was during the Civil War when it surrendered to Major-General Laugharne in 1645, but it escaped slighting. The present dilapidation dates from the eighteenth century, when the castle was owned by Lord Milford Haven. The first-floor chapel is well worth seeing and there are two fine undercrofts with barrel ceilings.

Lady Eaton. Open at Easter, the late Spring Bank Holiday to September.

Newcastle Emlyn

One solitary arch stands in a field on a bend in the river Teifi. Originally built by Prince Maredudd, of Llanstephan fame, it was captured by Edward I in 1288 when siege engines had pounded the walls. During the Glyndwr revolt it was captured and destroyed. Dafydd ap Gwilym, the Welsh poet, was brought up here when his uncle Llywelyn became constable in 1343. During the Civil War it held out for the king for some time but was completely slighted.

Ruins open at all reasonable times.

Newport

Built by Sir William de Martin in the eleventh century, Newport took over from Nevern as the seat of the Lord of Kemes. It passed to the Owens and for many years was a ruin until being restored in 1859 by Sir Thomas Lloyd, who converted the original entrance into a house, using the stones from the eastern gatehouse.

Mrs J. Hawkesworth. Not open to the public.

Pembroke

Built by Arnulf of Montgomery in 1090 at the end of a creek connected to Milford Haven, the first castle at Pembroke was a small timber and turf Norman fortress with the creek on one side and the river on the other. The first custodian, Gerald de Windsor, kept off the Welsh warriors of Cadwgan ab Bleddyn by cutting up four hogs and throwing the pieces to the enemy to convince them that they had ample supplies and could hold out until Arnulf came with assistance. Gerald later married the Welsh Princess Nesta who was able to keep the Welsh and Normans at peace by her beauty, in spite of the jealousy of Henry I. In 1138 Gilbert de Clare became the first Earl of Pembroke and he built the great keep which has walls 19 feet (5.8 m) thick at the base and rises to over 75 feet (23 m). It is now open to the top but once it had four storeys. Richard 'Strongbow', second Earl, used Pembroke as the base for his war against Ireland. His daughter Isabel married William Marshall, who became the next Earl and built the Norman hall and most of the castle which stands today. William's five sons succeeded him in turn and the last of them bequeathed the castle to his daughter, who married Warine de Munchensy. The northern hall was built at this time and was connected to the creek by a passage and staircase leading to the famous Wogan Cave.

Pembroke resisted the rising of Owain Glyndwr and the constable, Francis a'Court, paid a large levy to escape siege. In the fifteenth century Pembroke was held by Jasper Tudor and here the future Henry VII was born, son of the Earl of Richmond and Margaret Beaufort, Jasper's sister. He is supposed to have been born in a room in the tower now called after him and in 1471, after the Yorkist victory at Tewkesbury, Jasper and Henry and his mother escaped to Brittany. Fourteen years later Henry returned to Milford Haven with a small army and successfully captured the throne of England at Bosworth. Young Henry VIII was created Earl of Pembroke by his father, who looked upon the castle as his home.

The most famous period of Pembroke's long history, however, was during the Second Civil War in 1648. Three Parliamentarians, Major-General Laugharne, John Poyer, the mayor, and Colonel Powell, seemed to have enjoyed themselves and prospered so much during the First Civil War that they were very reluctant to disband. Poyer demanded his share of money for his services and when it was not forthcoming he shut himself up in the castle with his troops. Cromwell appointed Colonel Fleming as constable but some of Colonel Powell's men set on Fleming and drove him out of the town, capturing two culverins that had been landed from a ship in the harbour. In April 1648 there was a small battle between Powell and Fleming in which Fleming was killed and at this stage Laugharne, a brilliant soldier, arrived from London, where he had been held on suspicion of being involved in a Royalist plot. The Parliamentary commander Horton was at Cardiff with about three thousand men, and Laugharne and Powell raised a force of mixed Royalists, clubmen and disbanded Parliamentary soldiers of almost eight thousand. For a long time the battle that ensued at St Fagans on 8th May was in doubt but Okey's dragoons and the New Model infantry won the day and Laugharne and Powell retired to Pembroke. Cromwell arrived in person on 24th May and the siege lasted for seven weeks. The big guns opened up on 1st July but someone betrayed the water supply to Cromwell, who cut it off, and Laugharne was forced to surrender. Most of the rebels were set free but the three ringleaders were tried by Parliament and allowed to draw lots. The gallant mayor was taken to the Piazza in Covent Garden, where he was shot.

The inevitable slighting occurred and Pembroke remained a ruin until being partially restored in 1880 by J. R. Cobb of Brecon. The walk round the ramparts is rewarding and many of the towers have floors. The work of restoration continues.
Trustees of Pembroke Castle. Open throughout the year.

Picton

About 5 miles (8 km) south-west of Haverfordwest Picton Castle, built about 1190, was founded by William de Picton, a Norman knight. His descendants have occupied it ever since; the family name has been Philipps since 1425.

Picton Castle was besieged three times: in 1405 an invading French army, having unsuccessfully besieged Haverfordwest, came to Picton, which they took easily; in the Civil War Sir Richard Philipps was a Parliamentarian but the Royalists besieged and took his castle in 1643; it was retaken by Parliament in 1645. Subsequent generations have made alterations but the Norman castle remains basically unchanged. The grounds contain a fine collection of trees, flowering shrubs and other plants.
The Picton Castle Trust. Open Easter, Bank holidays, Sundays and Thursdays mid July to mid September.

Roch

A striking building with a tall tower, Roch Castle is 6 miles (10 km) north of Haverfordwest on A487. It was built by Adam de Rupe, according to legend, on a rock because he was afraid of adders, but one was brought into the castle with some firewood and killed him. In 1601 the Walters lived here and their daughter Lucy became the mistress of Charles II in The Hague. Her son was the luckless Duke of Monmouth. In 1900 Roch was restored by Viscount St David.

Privately owned. The castle and west wing may be hired for self-catering holidays.

Tenby

The castle above the harbour was built about 1153 but the few remaining pieces are of a later date. Tenby was sacked by Maelgwyn ap Rhys in 1187 and by Llywelyn ap Gruffydd in 1260. The town was strongly fortified at the time of the Armada. During the Civil War it was captured by Colonel Laugharne for Parliament and then in 1648 it was garrisoned by the Royalists and withstood another siege. Today it harbours a small museum of local history and nearby is a monument to Prince Albert.

Unrestricted access to ruins. Museum open throughout the year.

GWENT

Abergavenny

Founded by Hamelin of Ballon between 1087 and 1100, Abergavenny Castle was originally a timber structure on a mound surrounded by a stockade. The timber was later replaced by stone and a ditch was added on the north face towards the walled town. In Henry II's reign it passed to the de Braose family. William de Braose's uncle had been killed by Sitsyllt, Welsh leader of the Dyfnwal tribe, and in 1175 de Braose invited Sitsyllt and his warriors to a great feast. During the meal the Welsh were all put to death and William then took his murderous band to Sitsyllt's Castle Arnold nearby, where they murdered the leader's wife and son.

In Edward III's reign it was held by Lawrence de Hastings, who was created Earl of Pembroke and fought in the French wars. The widow of the last Lord Hastings married William de Beauchamp, who lived here during Glyndwr's rising. His constable was killed in 1402 by an angry mob, who rescued three townsmen from the gallows and imprisoned Lady Beauchamp in the keep. Later the castle passed to the Nevills. Charles I ordered the castle to be destroyed to prevent it from falling to the Scots in 1645.

The gatehouse of the castle dates from the fifteenth century and the 'keep' from 1819. It houses a very interesting small museum.

The Marquis of Abergavenny, leased to Monmouth District Council. Open throughout the year.

Caldicot

The impressive castle at Caldicot, which is a few miles west of Chepstow, between Caerwent and the Bristol Channel, was originally a motte and bailey castle built by Walter Fitzroger and his son Milo during the reign of Henry I. Milo's sons all died accidental deaths and Roger, who succeeded, became a monk. His son Walter, the Sheriff of Gloucester, also became a monk. Milo's daughter Margaret thus inherited Caldicot and it came to her husband, Humphrey de Bohun. The de Bohuns added the stone keep and the curtain walls. Humphrey, the fifth Earl of Hereford, was godfather to Prince Edward, son of Henry III, and this is the reason why he was pardoned after his capture at Evesham in 1265 when fighting for Simon de Montfort. The seventh Earl refused to go on a military expedition to Flanders in 1297 and, although the king threatened to execute him, he lived to become a champion of the baronial cause. The eighth Earl, whose coat of arms is above the massive castle gateway, married Elizabeth, daughter of Edward I. He was captured at Bannock-burn, and was exchanged only to die in 1322 at Boroughbridge. The ninth Earl was also prominent in the wars of the time and with his son fought against the French at Crecy. Finally the tenth Earl died young, leaving two daughters, Eleanor and Maria. The former married Thomas Woodstock, brother of John of Gaunt and the Black Prince. He added the Woodstock Tower and the main gatehouse in about 1385 but he opposed Richard II's marriage to Isabelle de Valois and was 'by the direction of the Earl Marshal, smothered between two feather beds'.

During the Wars of the Roses Caldicot was held by the Staffords, who were Yorkists. On the accession of Edward IV Caldicot was granted to William Herbert, Earl of Pembroke. He was killed after the battle of Edgecote and once more it was in the hands of the Crown. Henry VII restored it to the Staffords until Edward Stafford's execution for treason in 1521, when it became part of the Duchy of Lancaster. During the Civil War it was too decayed to be of much use as a stronghold and it was not until John R. Cobb purchased it in 1885 that it was repaired. His son G. Wheatley Cobb was the owner of Nelson's frigate *Foudroyant* and in the castle there are relics of the ship including the figurehead. Today the nineteenth-century banqueting hall can be leased for medieval banquets.

Open Easter to October.

Chepstow

Chepstow Castle is unusually placed. It is at the bottom of the hill by the river and not at the summit where it would have commanded the area. The first building was done by William Fitzosbern, Earl of Hereford, shortly after the Norman conquest. His great tower still stands — one of the finest remaining Norman keeps, altered and added to in height over the centuries. In 1075, Roger, son of William Fitzosbern, was disgraced for joining the Earls' Rising and it passed to the Crown. In 1115 the castle was granted to Walter Fitzrichard. In 1189 it passed by marriage to William Marshal. This great soldier and his four sons built most of the present castle, putting a curtain wall between the middle and lower baileys with circular towers at each end in which there are very early cross-shaped arrow slits. An unusual enclosure called the Barbican was added at the south-west corner and at the other end a strongly built outer bailey and main gatehouse were built.

Chepstow passed to the Bigods in 1248. Roger Bigod, Earl of Norfolk, built Marten's Tower in the outer bailey and his son added the western gatehouse in about 1272. The property passed to the Crown after Roger's death and thereafter was held by various constables including the Despencers and Thomas Mowbray, another Duke of Norfolk.

In 1468 William Herbert, Earl of Pembroke, owned Chepstow. It passed, on his granddaughter's marriage, to Charles, Earl of Worcester, whose family owned it until the twentieth century. A few windows and fireplaces were added at this time. During the Civil War the fifth Earl and first Marquess of Worcester held Chepstow for the king. In October 1645 it surrendered after a brief siege in spite of being held by a garrison of sixty-four men and seventeen guns. In 1648 Sir Nicholas Kemeys, who owned land in the area, supported Major General Laugharne and the valiant defenders of Pembroke. Cromwell sent Colonel Ewer from Gloucester to batter down the walls with his heavy siege train. A breach was made near Marten's Tower and many of the defenders escaped. Sir Nicholas failed to escape by boat and was caught and killed by Ewer's men.

The usual slighting did not take place and a permanent garrison remained at Chepstow until 1690 — the towers being used as a prison for Henry Marten, who was there for twenty years, and Jeremy Taylor, the Royalist bishop, who was imprisoned there during the Commonwealth. The garrison was removed in 1690 and the building fell into decay until 1953, when it was taken over by the Ministry of Works from the last owner, Mr D. R. Lysaght.

Cadw. Open throughout the year.

Grosmont

Grosmont, one of the three trilateral Gwent castles of the Welsh border, is built on a hill and can be reached by B4347 from Skenfrith and Monmouth. The original castle was built of wood and at the time of the Norman conquest belonged to one of the three sons of Prince Gwaethfoed. In the early thirteenth century the large two-storey hall was built and in about 1220 Hubert de Burgh added the gatehouse and towers, probably deepening the moat. Finally in 1330 an additional range of buildings outside the north curtain wall was built, including the tall surviving chimney. De Burgh's towers were destroyed by the Welsh, who attacked Grosmont at night in November 1233 and captured many of Henry III's supporters who had camped outside the moat, others escaping in their nightshirts. In 1405 Owain Glyndwr besieged the castle and burnt the village. Young Harry of Monmouth came to the rescue and defeated the besiegers, capturing one who, as he wrote to his father, was lately a 'great chieftain among them whom I would have sent up but that he is not yet able to ride at his ease'.

In Grosmont church is the effigy of a knight supposed to have been a descendant of Edmund Crouchback.

Cadw. Unrestricted access. Guide book obtainable from the post office.

Monmouth

The scanty ruins of Monmouth Castle, birthplace of Henry V, stand next to the impressive Great Castle House.

Open May to September.

Newport

The original castle here was Norman. Its successor was sacked by Glyndwr. The curtain wall and three towers standing beside the river Usk are mostly fourteenth-century work. The castle was used as a brewery for many years.

Cadw. Open throughout the year.

Penhow

Reputedly the oldest castle in Wales that is still inhabited, Penhow is in the process of complete restoration. Originally built in the thirteenth century by Sir William St Maur, whose name was changed to Seymour, it is the ancestral home of Edward Seymour, Protector to King Edward VI.

The Great Hall is upstairs and is connected by a narrow passage through the wall to another hall from which the tower stair rises to the bedchamber and the roof. There is a seventeenth-century dining room with a fine ceiling and an outside kitchen in process of restoration.

Mr S. Weeks. Open Easter to September, winter Wednesdays.

Raglan

Raglan is about halfway between Abergavenny and Monmouth on the A40. The present building, which is not so decayed as to be classed as a complete ruin, dates from the fifteenth century but is believed to stand on the site of a twelfth-century fortress. The Bloets owned the land from soon after the Norman conquest, but Sir James Berkeley acquired Raglan when he married Elizabeth Bloet. After his death she married William ap Thomas, who began the present castle.

Ap Thomas was knighted in 1426 and became Steward of Usk. He had a large retinue and to safeguard his new castle from gunpowder he built the six-sided Great Tower with its surrounding moat, known as the Yellow Tower of Gwent from the colour of the stone. It is a remarkable piece of architecture and originally had an extra storey with battlements, matching the other two towers of Raglan. On the ground floor the arrow loops are combined with gunports and there was a double drawbridge. Vertical grooves in the side of the tower were for the beams of the single and double drawbridges so that when closed they were flush with the tower. The only similar drawbridge to this is in Milan.

The next owner, William Herbert, son of ap Thomas, was a prominent Yorkist and adviser to Edward IV. He was created Earl of Pembroke and constructed the main castle building round a courtyard known as Fountain Court. Herbert was executed after his defeat at Edgcote in 1469 and his son inherited Raglan. Through his daughter Elizabeth the castle passed to Sir Charles Somerset, Lord Chamberlain to both Henry VII and Henry VIII. His son William was a patron of Elizabethan drama and rebuilt the Pitched Stone Court. The hall was raised in height and an office building was erected next to the kitchen tower. A long gallery was built over the chapel and buttery so that by 1589, when Somerset, who was the third Earl of Worcester, died, he left behind a fortified Elizabethan manor. Edward, the fourth Earl, was responsible for the niches in the wall round the Yellow Tower, which once contained statues.

The fifth Earl, created Marquess of Worcester, was reputed to be the richest man in England and much of his fortune went to supporting the Royalist cause in the Civil War. His son, Lord Herbert, constructed a water engine at Raglan which made 'a fearful and hideous noise' and was used to great effect to drive away local men who came in search of arms. Charles I stayed at Raglan on more than one occasion and in 1646 the castle was besieged by a strong force of Parliamentarians, led at the end by Fairfax, so that the Marquess, after a desperate fight, finally surrendered on 19th August. 'The house almost starved . . . had like to have eaten one another' was the report and the Parliamentarians called in the local people to help demolish the Marquess's home.

Cadw. Open throughout the year.

Skenfrith

Not far from Monmouth at the junction of B4347 and B4521 stands Skenfrith Castle, another of the trilateral castles built beside the river Monnow to defend the Welsh border. Originally there was a motte in a rectangular enclosure, which was protected by a bank and a ditch and which measured about 700 by 400 feet (210 by 120 m) and included the church. It was a village enclosure on which the tower was built.

In 1201 Skenfrith was granted to Hubert de Burgh by King John and he probably built the keep and held it with Grosmont and White Castle until 1232, except for a brief period early on when it was held by William de Braose. In 1232 the Crown requisitioned the three castles, keeping them until 1254, when Skenfrith passed to Henry III's son Prince Edward. In 1267 Edward gave all three to his younger brother Edmund Crouchback. Skenfrith remained part of the Duchy of Lancaster until passing to Mr Harold Sands, who presented it to the National Trust in 1936.

The castle is primitive in design, consisting of a two-storey tower on the motte, originally possessing an outside staircase, and a quadrangular curtain wall with five circular towers. There are traces of a moat on the south and west sides and the river flows so close to the east side that the river gate has had to be blocked due to floods. Inside the church, with its half-timbered tower, is the monument to John Morgan, governor of the castle in the sixteenth century.

National Trust and Cadw. Open at all times. Guide book obtainable from the post office.

Usk

The best view of Usk Castle is from the church looking up at the hill. It stands on private property up a lane by the fire station. It has two towers and a square keep and dates largely from the fourteenth century. The castle was built by the de Clares about 1100 and passed to the Mortimer family. It was destroyed by Owain Glyndwr, repaired and finally reduced to its present state in the Civil War.

Mr and Mrs R. H. J. Humphreys. Grounds open once a year under the National Gardens Scheme. Castle ruins not open.

White Castle

Near Abergavenny off B4521 or B4233, White or Llantilio Castle is, with Grosmont and Skenfrith, one of the trilateral Norman castles built to secure Gwent. The first known owner was Pain Fitzjohn, a soldier of Henry I's army. The first structure on this remote hill was probably a wooden tower, which was replaced before the beginning of the thirteenth century by a rectangular stone keep surrounded by a curtain enceinte. The owner was then William de Braose and later his son, who gained control over the castle during the troubled last years of King John's reign.

The main building of the castle dates from about 1263, when Prince Edward strengthened his border fortress against the threat of Llywelyn ap Gruffydd. The main entrance was 'ransferred from the south to the north, which explains the hornwork in the moat that originally protected the first entrance into the keep. An outer ward was constructed with thick palisaded banks.

There appears to have been no siege or battle at White Castle and unlike Grosmont and Skenfrith its buildings were purely of military nature. It was used as a rent collecting centre and as a mustering point for the war against the Scots. It belonged to the Duchy of Lancaster until the accession of Henry IV, when it became Crown property. In 1825 it was sold to the Duke of Beaufort. In 1902 it was acquired by Sir Henry Mather Jackson and in 1922 it passed to the Ministry of Public Building and Works, which carried out repairs and built the gatehouse stair and platform.

During the Second World War an occasional visitor to the castle was Rudolf Hess, who, after his flight to Scotland, was kept in an Abergavenny mental home.

Cadw. Open throughout the year.

GWYNEDD

Beaumaris

The finest preserved concentric castle in Britain, Beaumaris is on the Anglesey coast overlooking Lavan sands and the north-east end of the Menai Strait. When Caernarfon was captured by the Welsh in 1294 during the Welsh uprising Edward I decided to protect the harbour and ferry at the other end of the strait and began to build a new castle in 1295. It was completed in 1298. The garrison consisted of ten men-at-arms, twenty bowmen and one hundred foot soldiers. The upper storeys of the two gatehouses, the Great Hall and other internal buildings were never completed. Some further building of the curtain wall was carried out in 1306 and a few years later the north gate was strengthened.

The extensive dock is at the southern side of the curtain and is protected by a bastion called the Gunners' Walk, in which the castle watermill was situated. There was a drawbridge connecting the dock to the castle and a 40 ton ship could moor at the gate. There appears to be no well in the castle so there may have been some system of piping water in from a stream, which would have been difficult with a sea moat round the outer ward, or of conserving rainwater.

One of the constables of Beaumaris was Henry Hotspur, who met his death at the battle of Shrewsbury in 1403. During the Civil War the Royalist commander, Colonel Bulkeley, surrendered on 14th June 1646 and the castle somehow escaped slighting. During the 1648 campaign Bulkeley raised a force in Beaumaris to aid the Scots but after Preston he had little hope of success. In September a Parliamentary force of about fifteen hundred man, commanded by General Mytton, crossed the strait. Bulkeley occupied a position near the almshouses on the Beaumaris-Pentraeth road. A scrappy, confused battle took place here on 1st October, in which Mytton suffered about forty casualties and the Royalists thirty with about three hundred men captured. Bulkeley and his second in command, Colonel Whiteley, shut themselves up in the castle but Mytton said he would kill the prisoners if the two did not surrender. For a short time Bulkeley was imprisoned but he was allowed to ransom himself and eventually escaped to Europe.

Cadw. Open throughout the year.

Belan Fort

At Llanwnda, on the south tip of the Menai Strait, this fort was built in 1776 and strengthened in 1826. It was manned by the Royal Newborough Volunteers.

Fort Belan has its own private dock and is worth visiting for the maritime museum, forge, speedboat rides and cannon firing. *Open May to September.*

Castell y Bere

Tucked away at the top of the Dysynni valley about 8 miles (13 km) from Tywyn, Castell y Bere gives the impression of once being an island fortress now surrounded by land. Nearby is Bird Rock, the only inland nesting ground for cormorants in this area. The ruin consists of a few stones, dating from the thirteenth century, arranged in two parts, the south section having a postern gate protected by a drum tower. It was a stronghold of Llywelyn the Great and later of his brother Dafydd. Eventually captured by the Earl of Pembroke, it fell into decay. *Cadw. Unrestricted access.*

Caernarfon

The Romans first built a fort here called *Segontium* or Y Gaer yn Arfor, which was the original settlement on the Beddgelert road and the river Seiont. The first castle on the present site was built about 1090 by Earl Hugh of Avranches and consisted of a large motte with timber walls. The bailey was probably what is now Castle Square.

In 1282 Llywelyn ap Gruffydd (the Last) was killed attacking Builth Castle and Edward I captured Dolwyddelan Castle, ensuring his control of North Wales. In the summer of 1283 work started on the present castle, which encircles Hugh's motte. Work ceased in 1292, although the castle appears never to have been finished.

In April 1284 Edward I's second son was born at Caernarfon and in 1301, after his elder brother had died, young Edward was formally presented to the Welsh people as their Prince of Wales. Tradition states that this event took place at Caernarfon but it is more likely that it was at the older castle of Rhuddlan. In 1294 Madoc ap Llywelyn's revolt destroyed the town walls and the wooden buildings of the castle were burnt. The following year the damage was repaired and the town-side castle walls were built up to their present height. It was at this time that the multiple arrow loops were put in by the Granary Tower so that three men could shoot through each slit in different directions at the same time. In 1304 there was another fire and damage had to be repaired.

In 1660 orders were given for the complete demolition of the castle. The work was never started, perhaps because of lack of finance, and in the nineteenth century prosperity came to the port with the increase in the slate trade. Sir Llewelyn Turner, Deputy Constable, repaired much of the stonework, rebuilt the top of the Well Tower and, using sandstone, added a great deal of character to the castle.

Apart from the multangular towers, the passages inside the walls and the visual splendour of the castle, the most interesting item for visitors is the Royal Welsh Fusiliers' Museum in the Queen's Tower. Here one can see, on three floors, four Victoria Crosses, numerous flags, the keys of Corunna, medals of Waterloo veterans, First and Second World War relics and the silver cigarette case of Major Compton-Smith DSO, which he presented to the regiment on the night before he was shot by the Sinn Feiners when captured in Ireland in 1920.

Caernarfon has been the scene of two royal investitures — Prince Edward, later the Duke of Windsor, in 1911, and Prince Charles in 1969. Perhaps before there is a third investiture, the work started by Edward I will finally be completed.

Cadw. Open throughout the year.

Conwy

Although the mouth of the Afon Conwy was a natural position for a castle, the earliest castle in the area was at Deganwy overlooking the estuary. Edward I, having captured Dolwyddelan, moved to Conwy in 1283 and James of St George was given the task of building the great castle at the river mouth. Much of the material from ruined Deganwy was used in its making. By 1287 it was complete. Within two years it was fit for a garrison and in 1294, during Prince Madoc's rising, Edward was besieged here and had to be rescued by his fleet.

A hundred years later Richard II received the Duke of Northumberland here as an emissary from Henry Bolingbroke. Richard set out for Flint and for his downfall. During the Wars of the Roses Conwy held out for the Yorkists and a Lancastrian, Rhys ap Gruffydd Goch, was said to have been killed at a range of half a mile (800 m) by an arrow shot by the Yorkist marksman, Llewelyn of Nannau.

By 1627 the castle had fallen into decay and was sold for £100 to Viscount Conway. In the Civil War, Bishop John Williams refortified it for the king. Conwy town walls were strengthened. Sir John Owen, who did not trust the bishop, took over the command of the castle. Major-General Mytton attacked and captured the town in August 1646. He then turned his artillery on the castle to little effect and Owen held out until November when his men marched out on favourable terms, secured for the most part by the bishop. After the Restoration it fell into disrepair again and has been roofless since Lord Conway sold the roof lead in 1665.

During the nineteenth century the railway company was prevailed upon to repair the stonework, which had suffered from the constant shaking by freight trains, and John Parker of Oxford restored the floors of the high tower at his own expense, so that 'visitors could come and sit and sketch'. In 1865 Sir Richard Bulkeley, the last constable appointed by the Queen, died and the castle passed to the local corporation. In 1953 it was taken over by the Ministry and the Telford bridge, built in 1826, was acquired by the National Trust in 1966.

Cadw. Open throughout the year. National Trust information centre in toll house.

Criccieth

Criccieth is a small seaside resort on the A497 to Pwllheli. The castle stands high above the bay and was probably built by Llywelyn ap Iowerth, who imprisoned his half-brother Gruffydd here in 1239. The inner ward with its two drum towers dates from 1230. The outer ward with its rectangular towers dates from about 1290, when Edward I strengthened it, making the inner gatehouse higher, and refaced the Cistern Tower, which is common to both inner and outer wards.

In 1284 Edward I appointed William de Leyburn as constable with a garrison of thirty men. In 1343 it belonged to the Black Prince. The constable at this time was Sir Hywel ap Gruffydd, a redoubtable warrior nicknamed 'Howell of the Battleaxe', who was knighted on the field of Poitiers. There are traces of fire, particularly on the Leyburn Tower, which probably date from the castle's destruction by Owain Glyndwr in 1404. The castle has not been inhabited since then. In 1933 Lord Harlech placed the castle in state guardianship.

Cadw. Open throughout the year.

Dolbadarn

On A4086 between the two small lakes of Llyn Padarn and Llyn Peris, Dolbadarn Castle stands 80 feet (24 m) above on a small rock. There are remains of a curtain wall that enclosed an area of about 12,000 square feet (1100 sq m). The road once ran very close to the castle to avoid a swamp. Originally Dolbadarn was a stronghold built by the Welsh to guard the valley.

The circular tower, well preserved today, dates from the thirteenth century and may have been built by Llywelyn Fawr (the Great). Traditionally his grandson Llywelyn ap Gruffydd held his brother prisoner here for nearly twenty years. On Llywelyn's death at Builth in 1282 Dolbadarn passed into Edward I's hands and henceforward ceased to be of importance. In 1284 parts of it were dismantled and the timber was used for the construction of Caernarfon. During Owain Glyndwr's rising Dolbadarn was the prison of Lord Grey of Ruthin but it is unlikely that it was used for warfare after this time.

The last owner, Sir Michael Duff, presented it to the Ministry of Works in 1941 and a great deal of repointing, clearing and repair work has been carried out since this date.

Cadw. Open throughout the year.

Dolwyddelan

On A496 between Betws-y-Coed and Blaenau Ffestiniog, the tall tower of Dolwyddelan Castle stands out overlooking the road. It is famous as the presumed birthplace and early home of Llywelyn the Great. When Owain Gwynnedd died his sons divided up North Wales and Llywelyn's father Iowerth, who died in about 1173, when his son was born, ruled over Nant Conwy with Dolwyddelan tower as his headquarters.

In 1283 the English captured Dolwyddelan on their successful campaign in North Wales and it was repaired. In the fifteenth century it belonged to Meredydd ap Ieuan, a descendant of Llywelyn, and on his death it fell into decay. The roof and battlements were added in the nineteenth century and the Ministry of Works took over care of the castle in 1930.

The castle originally had two towers and a stone curtain with a ditch on the east and another to the west. The old road passed under the west tower at one time. The keep is constructed in the

English style with the entrance on the first floor up a steep staircase interrupted by a drawbridge pit. The basement was entered by a ladder and the main living quarters must have been the one room, now much restored, with its window seats and chimney. At one time there was a gabled roof. There are few castles in Wales so well looked after as Dolwyddelan.
Cadw. Open throughout the year.

Harlech

Harlech is Edward I's most magnificently situated castle. It stands on a rock overlooking the sea with its enormous gatehouse on the town side compactly set in the east wall and guarded by the four huge circular corner towers and the high curtain. It was built by Edward I between 1283 and 1289, coming under siege in 1294 when Madoc ap Llywelyn unsuccessfully attacked. Owain Glyndwr next attacked it in 1401 and for four years it was an English outpost in hostile country. Finally worn out by disease and desertion the garrison was bribed to surrender by Glyndwr. For four years the Welsh leader used it as his home. In 1408 after a short siege it was captured by the Talbots' army of a thousand men equipped with siege engines that fired huge cannonballs, one of which was 22 inches (560 mm) in diameter.

During the Wars of the Roses, Harlech held out for the Lancastrians until 14th August 1468, when Dafydd ap Ieuan and his 'Men of Harlech' were confronted by the Earl of Pembroke, his brother, Sir Richard Herbert, and their 'Saxons', and the castle fell. During the Civil War it was held for the king, finally surrendering to Colonel Mytton in 1647. Unlike Rhuddlan and Pembroke it was never slighted and Cromwell used it as a jail for the Scots captured at Dunbar.
Cadw. Open throughout the year.

MID GLAMORGAN

Caerphilly

The largest castle in Wales and one of the largest in the British Isles, Caerphilly lies 7 miles (11 km) north of Cardiff on A469. Its site immediately adjoins a Roman fort. The Welsh controlled the area until 1266, when Earl Gilbert of Gloucester, who had helped Henry III overthrow Simon de Montfort, attacked Gruffydd ap Rhys and confiscated his land. To secure his conquests he started a vast building programme but before a year was out Llywelyn attacked and damaged what had been built. By 1272 Gilbert had built a fortress surrounded by a lake. It had two entrances, a large western hornwork and a central inner ward similar to Harlech, but covering a larger area. The main entrance, on the east or town side, has a platform on each side behind an outer moat with a water gate — the whole making a fortress that must have been practically impregnable.

In 1326-7, during the reign of Edward II, the castle was besieged by Queen Isabella. After the king had been captured, terms were agreed and the garrison marched out. Edward IV granted the castle to the Earl of Pembroke. During the Civil War a large earthwork was built in the north-west corner, over the Roman fort. There was no siege and the slighting that took place in 1646 was believed to be a Royalist precaution to prevent a resident garrison from being inflicted on the town. The towers were probably blown up by gunpowder and one of them has been leaning precariously ever since.

The Marquess of Bute did some restoration in the 1930s and the main entrance bridge was repaired in 1958.
Cadw. Open throughout the year.

Coity

Coity Castle is a few miles north of Bridgend; it has a circular inner ward with a moat to the north, east and south and an outer ward on the west side. The square keep has Norman outer walls but was rebuilt internally in the fourteenth century. Much of the curtain wall of the inner ward is late twelfth-century, though the northern section was rebuilt in the fourteenth century. The inner ward contains the domestic buildings.

Coity was the home of the Turbervilles for three centuries. According to tradition Payn de Turbeville received Coity after the conquest of Glamorgan and confirmed his possession by marrying the daughter of the last Welsh owner.

When the last of the Turbevilles died in Edward III's reign the castle passed through marriage to Sir Roger Berkerolles. When his son died the new owner was Sir William Gamage, who held out in a long siege against Owain Glyndwr. Barbara, the last of the Gamage family, married Robert Sidney, brother of the famous Sir Philip, who was responsible for the Tudor apartments in the inner ward and the windows in the hall.
Cadw. Open throughout the year.

Newcastle

On the west of the river Ogmore, near Bridgend, Newcastle has a Norman castle which consists of a small piece of curtain wall and a gateway. Like Coity it belonged to the Turbervilles, Gamages and Sidneys. In 1718 it was bought by Samuel Edwin of Llanfihangel and then it passed to the Dunraven estate.

The richly carved Norman gateway is unusual and was often thought to have been taken from a church. There is no evidence for this and the doorway has been dated at 1175, which might explain the name Newcastle. It is probable that it was built after Coity.

Cadw. Open throughout the year.

Ogmore

Near the mouth of the Ogmore river, the ruins are reached over stepping stones by the Pelican Inn. The keep was first mentioned in 1106 and had three storeys. The probable builder was Gwilim O'Lundein. A vaulted passage leads to another rectangular building opposite, which is a fifteenth-century courthouse.

Open daily. Key from nearby farmhouse.

POWYS

Brecon

Brecon Castle stands high above the bridge over the Usk. The castle dates from 1090 when Bernard de Neufmarché built a motte and bailey with stones taken from the Roman camp of Gaer. Remains of these are in the Deanery garden. Brecon successfully withstood two sieges by Llywelyn the Great in 1216 and 1233. It was occupied by Henry IV and defended by one hundred men-at-arms and three hundred archers who received one shilling and sixpence per day respectively.

Charles I came to Brecon after Naseby. By then parts of the castle had been dismantled by townsfolk, so that it could not be fortified. The main part of the castle has been attached to the Castle Hotel and can be seen from the garden.

Postcards and permission to see the outside of the castle should be obtained from the Castle Hotel. The interior is not open. Bishop Moreton's Ely Tower is opposite.

Bronllys

Between Brecon and Hay, on the banks of the Lynfi, Bronllys Tower is 80 feet (24 m) high and has two passages inside the wall. It is of early Norman date. Used as a base by William Rufus, it later passed to the Bohuns and in the reign of Henry VII to the Staffords.

Cadw. Open October to April. Key obtainable from Bronllys House.

Crickhowell

A ruin is all that remains of Alisby's castle, destroyed in 1403 by Owain Glyndwr. The archers from Crickhowell were famous in Edward I's army.

Hay-on-Wye

Hay is situated on the border with England. The word 'Hay' is from the French *haie*, meaning an enclosure. The first castle was a motte and bailey near the church. The Norman castle was constructed by Phillip Walwyn and afterwards passed to William Revell, who presented land to form the parish in 1130. The next owners were the de Braose family and William de Braose rebelled against King John. His wife Maud de Valerie refused to give up her sons as hostages to the king and accused him of murdering his nephew Arthur. For this she was thrown into the dungeons of Corfe Castle, where she died.

During Owain Glyndwr's rebellion the castle and town were destroyed and only the gateway and one tower remain. In Elizabethan times a mansion was built next door.

Richard Booth Esq. Not open to the public.

Montgomery

Montgomery Castle was constructed to replace Hen Domen Castle, remains of which can still be seen by the former railway station. Baldwin de Boller built his new castle on the hill above the town in Henry I's reign and this was enlarged in 1223 and became the home of the Herberts. Lord Herbert of Chirbury, brother of George Herbert, the poet, decided in 1622 to build a house inside the middle ward and it was reputedly a splendid, richly furnished mansion. (The staircase still survives at Aldborough Hall, North Yorkshire.)

During the Civil War the Herberts handed over the castle to Sir Thomas Myddelton in 1644 and the Royalists promptly besieged the castle. Reinforced by Sir William Fairfax, brother of Thomas, Myddelton beat off Byron's attack and in spite of Fairfax being mortally wounded the Roundheads won the day. Montgomery Castle was demolished in 1649 by order of Parliament.

Excavations in 1973 revealed remains of Lord Herbert's house and the garrison rooms of the castle together with a deep well. They also revealed that Montgomery had a gatehouse with twin D-shaped drum towers, one of the first castles to have these, which became a characteristic of Edward I's great Welsh castles.

Cadw. Open throughout the year.

Powis

Just south-west of Welshpool, Powis was built at the end of the thirteenth century to command the upper Severn valley. It has been in continuous occupation since the day it was built and was altered in the seventeenth and nineteenth centuries. The first builder was Gruffydd, Baron de la Pole, who supported Edward I. His family died out in 1551 and in 1587 Sir Edward Herbert purchased the estate and was responsible for building the Long Gallery, although much work was carried out by Sir John Cherlton, who married the heiress of the de la Poles. During the Civil War Powis was captured by Sir Thomas Myddelton for Parliament and during the Commonwealth it was occupied by the Welshpool Committee. Sir Edward's grandson finally returned in 1667 and repaired the damage to the interior, putting in much of the panelling. He built the west gate used by visitors today and the state bedroom.

William III granted Powis to his nephew, the Earl of Rochford, who was responsible for building the Dutch style terraces with their statues of shepherds and shepherdesses by Van Nost. Lanscroom was brought in to paint the great staircase.

In 1722 the son of the exiled Marquess of Powis was reinstated. His son succeeded him and in 1748 Henry Herbert, who had fought in the Culloden campaign and had been made a general, married the niece of the Marquess and became Earl of Powis. His daughter married Lord Clive, Governor of Madras, and son of the victor of Plassey. In 1804 he was created Earl of Powis and his son changed his name to Herbert.

National Trust. Open regularly April to November; Sundays November to March.

Tretower

After the conquest of the region by Bernard de Newmarch in the late eleventh century, one of his knights, Sir Miles Picard, built a motte and bailey castle at Tretower, which was called Stradewy until the early fifteenth century. His grandson, John, probably built the stone-walled shell keep in the late twelfth century, containing a hall, solar and kitchen. Roger Picard, in the thirteenth century, built the great tower on the site of the hall and solar and strengthened the walls of the keep, and the bailey was enclosed by a curtain wall. The castle was again garrisoned and refurnished during Owain Glyndwr's rebellion in 1403.

The nearby manor house, Tretower Court, originally built by the Picards about 1300, was granted to Sir Roger Vaughan by William Herbert, Earl of Pembroke, in 1450. Sir Roger began rebuilding the court in its present form, his son Thomas completing the work. It was modernised about 1630 by Charles Vaughan.

Cadw. Court and castle open throughout the year.

SOUTH GLAMORGAN

Cardiff

Originally a Roman fort, Cardiff Castle was built to defend the

Taff estuary. In 1091 the Normans used the same site for their motte and surrounding moat built by Robert Fitzhamon. The Welsh leader Ivor Bach captured the Norman stronghold in 1158. The buildings that remain today on top of the motte are chiefly twelfth-century and were erected by Robert, Duke of Gloucester. Gilbert de Clare made additions in the thirteenth century and also constructed a wall across to the Black Tower, thus creating two baileys. Further building took place in Tudor times along the west wall and the outer curtain was built up to the probable Roman height.

The last of the de Clares was killed at Bannockburn and the castle was acquired by the Despencers, favourites of Edward II, and later by the Earls of Warwick. On the death of Richard Neville, 'Warwick the Kingmaker', at the battle of Barnet in 1471, it passed to Anne Neville, who married the Duke of Gloucester, who became Richard III. In the sixteenth century it passed to the Earl of Pembroke and then to Viscount Windsor. The third Marquess of Bute was responsible for the massive Victorian additions. His architect, William Burges, built the tall Clock Tower, the Guest Tower and the Octagonal Tower spire and completely redesigned the interior in the current medieval romantic style, similar to Castell Coch. In 1947 the castle was presented to the citizens of Cardiff.

Cardiff City Council. Open daily except Christmas Day, Boxing Day and New Year's Day.

Castell Coch

William Burges's nineteenth-century castle stands in a wood near Tongwynlais, about half a mile (800 m) from the A470 Cardiff to Pontypridd road. The Marquess of Bute hired William Burges in 1872 to prepare plans for rebuilding a thirteenth-century ruin, once the home of the de Clares, that stood on a natural shelf overlooking the river Taff. Burges decided that the original building had been constructed in two periods, the first with red sandstone, the second with ashlar. Using the old base he built three circular towers with a roofed Elizabethan-style gallery forming the inner court. He used conical roofs on the theory that in medieval times they would have kept out arrows and the site was unsuitable for siege engines.

The enthusiast for Victoriana should not miss Castell Coch. *Cadw. Open throughout the year.*

Old Beaupre

Just off A48 near the village of St Hilary, down an un-signposted lane near the church, is the ruin of the sixteenth-century manor house of the Basset family. It was only partially castellated, having an outer gatehouse and crenellated curtain

walls, and fell into decay when Sir Richard Basset lost his money as a Royalist in the Civil War.
Cadw. Open throughout the year.

St Donat's

The first known owners of St Donat's Castle were the Stradlings, who came here in 1297 and intermarried with the de Haweys, who then owned the land where the massive, well restored castle now stands on the coast near Llantwit Major. The early part of the building dates from 1300 and the Great Hall from Elizabethan times. During the Civil War Sir Edward Stradling, his brothers and sons went off to fight for the king and Lady Stradling was left behind in the castle but it was never attacked, partly because St Donat's commands no main road and can be easily bypassed. The last Stradling was killed in a duel in France by his friend Sir John Tyrrwhitt, whose family then obtained the castle in 1755 and allowed it to become ruinous. It was restored by Dr Carne in 1862 and further by Morgan Williams, an American coal-owner in 1901.

In 1925 William Randolph Hearst, the American newspaper owner, hired Sir Charles Allom to put the castle in order. Bedrooms were increased from three to thirty-five, central heating was installed, and parts of a ruined Wiltshire priory were moved to St Donat's. During the Second World War St Donat's was occupied by the army and in 1962 it became Atlantic College, with 360 students from all over the world. Today it is the best preserved inhabited castle in Wales.
Atlantic College. Open June and July, weekday afternoons.

St Fagan's

The castle here was built by the Normans and changed hands many times, once being sold by the Herberts to raise money for Sir Walter Raleigh's expedition to Guiana. There was a battle here in 1648 when General Horton defeated the Royalists. The present ruins are sixteenth-century and the site is now the Welsh Folk Museum.
National Museum of Wales. Open throughout the year.

WEST GLAMORGAN

Loughor

Off the main Swansea-Llanelli road, Loughor Tower is all that remains of a Norman castle destroyed in 1151 by Rhys ap Gruffydd. Some of its masonry is of a later date.
Cadw. Unrestricted access.

Oxwich

Built by the Mansels in the sixteenth century, Oxwich is a fortified manor at the top of a winding lane a mile from Oxwich beach. The building is partly used as a farm and is in need of restoration. Sir Rice Mansel built his house in 1541 on the site of a Norman fort. In 1557 a ship was wrecked at Oxwich and Sir George Herbert of Swansea claimed the contents. Sir Rice and his son Edward had, however, already helped themselves to most of the spoils and when Herbert's men protested a fight ensued in which a stone hit and killed Anne Mansel in her own doorway, which still carries the family coat of arms.
Not open to the public.

Oystermouth

Between Swansea and Mumbles there is a small thirteenth-century castle which stands high up in a park a few minutes walk inland from the beach. The original castle at Oystermouth was built in 1100 and destroyed in 1215 and was abandoned by the owner, William de Londres. It was rebuilt by William de Braose but was burnt again by the Welsh. Edward I stayed here in 1284 and three years later the Welsh attacked it again. The gatehouse and curtain walls were added and the rectangular keep strengthened. Today it presents a compact and remarkably complete structure, unique amongst Welsh castles.
Open regularly during the summer.

Penard

This is a thirteenth-century ruin overlooking Three Cliffs Bay. It consists of a curtain wall and a piece of the great hall. The castle was excavated in 1961 and four chambers were revealed, the hall, private rest room and two storerooms. The ruins were reburied and the sand has encroached on the remaining stones.
Penard Cliff belongs to the National Trust.

Weobley

On the north coast of Gower near Landimore, Weobley is a fortified manor house dating from the thirteenth and fourteenth centuries. It stands on a grassy hill overlooking Llanrhidian sands and was originally built about 1300 by the de la Bere family. It passed to Sir Rhys ap Thomas, the Herberts and the Mansels. It was damaged in 1409 by Owain Glyndwr and in Henry VIII's reign it belonged to Lady Catherine Edgecumbe. The last owner was Miss Talbot of Penrice, who gave it to the Ministry of Works in 1911. The hall still possessed a roof at this time as it had been used as a farmhouse, but today only the forebuilding is roofed over.
Cadw. Open throughout the year.

Glossary

Arrow-slit: a long narrow opening for firing arrows through. To accommodate crossbows they had small holes at the end of the slit or were cross-shaped with holes. After the fourteenth century they became gunports.

Bailey: the castle courtyard or ward. There were inner and outer baileys, each with a separate gate, and sometimes with a second drawbridge connecting the inner to the outer bailey.

Ballista: a large bow for shooting missiles (iron bolts). It was reasonably accurate and led to the mini-ballista or crossbow.

Barbican: the gateway, watchtower or outwork defending the drawbridge.

Bartisan: a small overhanging turret projecting from an angle. Usually placed on top of a tower or battlements.

Bastion: a small tower at the end of a curtain wall or in the middle of an outside wall.

Bastle: a rectangular two-storey building with an outside stair used for defence by northern smallholders. The stock would be shut in on the ground floor and the occupants on the first floor.

Batter: the sloping part of the wall, usually at the bottom of the curtain so that rocks and missiles dropped from the battlements will hit the batter and bounce on to the besiegers.

Battlement: a wall or parapet on top of a building with embrasures or identations with raised portions between. Also called crenellations.

Belfry: a tall wooden tower with stages and covered in hides that was moved up by attackers to obtain access to the parapet. It was sometimes equipped with a base for a battering ram.

Berm: the flat space between the base of the curtain wall and the inner edge of the moat or ditch.

Bore: an iron-tipped pole used for making holes in the base of a castle wall.

Brattice: the wooden hoarding constructed on and overhanging the crenellations and fitted with a roof to protect the defenders. Missiles could be thrown from a brattice at anyone attempting to scale or undermine the walls.

Cabalus: a type of trebuchet.

Caponiere: a covered passage often used to connect one part of a fort to another or to protect an entrance as at Hurst.

Crenellation: *see* Battlement. The licence to crenellate was a permit from the Crown to fortify a house or to build a castle.

Curtain: the wall or rampart enclosing a courtyard. Bastions were sometimes placed at intervals along it.

Donjon: the strong central tower or keep to which the garrison retired when hard pressed — from the Latin *dominionem* meaning 'with the lordship'. Dungeon is the same word but now has a different meaning.

Drawbridge: a wooden bridge that can be raised towards a gateway. Usually placed over a moat.

Embrasure: a door or window with inside slanting sides. Later used as a gunport.

Enceinte: an enclosure; the area of a fortified place.

Forebuilding: an additional building next to the keep in which the chapel and a stair to the keep entrance were often situated.

Garderobe: the latrine. Often situated off the tower stair and cut into the wall.

Hoards or Hourdes: brattices. The holes for the supporting timbers are often clearly visible today.

Keep: the donjon or strong central tower.

Machicolation: the projecting stone parapet or gallery with openings through which the defenders could pour molten substances or missiles on the attackers. The word also applied to the openings themselves.

Malvoisin: a 'bad neighbour' or large earth or stone mound thrown up by the attackers near the wall of a castle from which they could fire into the wards or bailey.

Mangonel: a stone-throwing engine working on the torsion principle.

Merlon: part of a battlement wall between two embrasures or crenellations.

Motte: an eleventh- or twelfth-century mound of earth on the edge of the bailey.

Newel: a stair built in a spiral form with the steps keyhole-shaped to fit on top of each other and descending clockwise.

Petraria: stone-throwing engine. Could be a mangonel, ballista or trebuchet.

Portcullis: an iron or wooden grille gate with spikes that was raised and lowered in vertical grooves in front of the main gate. There were sometimes two or three to pass under (as well as machicolations) before one reached the keep.

Postern: a back door or a covered passage between the main ditch and outworks of a fort, guarded by a postern gate.

Rampart: the surrounding wall or raised earthwork. (Hence a ram was used to batter down a rampart or rampart gate.)

Ravelin: a detached earthwork with two embankments.

Sap: the undermining of a wall.

Slight: to destroy a castle in such a way as to render it useless for fortification.

Solar: the parlour or lord's private apartment. Usually on the first floor with access by a private stair.

Springall: *see* Ballista.

Trebuchet: more powerful than the mangonel, it was a stone-throwing engine worked on the counterweight principle.

Turning bridge: a wooden bridge pivoted on an axle fitted with a counterweight on the end nearest the gateway.

Vice: a spiral turret stair commonly found in a keep. The handrail was carved out of the outside wall so the defender, when descending, had his right hand free for his weapon.

Ward: *see* Bailey.

Yett: an iron grille on hinges. A common form of gate in a Scottish castle.

Bibliography

Armitage, E. S. *Early Norman Castles of the British Isles*. John Murray, 1912.

Braun, Hugh. *The English Castle*. Batsford, second edition 1942.

Edwards, J. Goronwy. *Edward I's Castle Building in Wales*. British Academy Reprint, 1944.

Fry, Plantagenet Somerset. *The David and Charles Book of Castles*. David and Charles 1980.

Hatt, E. M., and Sharp, Paul. *British Castles, Follies and Monuments*. Reprint Society, 1960.

Oman, Charles. *Castles*. Great Western Railway, 1926.

O'Neil, B. H. St J. *Castles*. HMSO, 1954.

Renn, Derek. *Norman Castles in Britain*. John Baker, 1968.

Simpson, W. Douglas. *Castles in England and Wales*. Batsford, 1969.

Thompson, A. Hamilton. *Military Architecture in England during the Middle Ages*. Oxford University Press, 1912.

Timbs, J., and Gunn, A. *Abbeys, Castles and Ancient Halls of England and Wales, North, Midland and South*. Warne, 1930.

Toy, Sidney. *Castles of Great Britain*. Heinemann, 1953.

See also *English Heritage Guide*, *English Heritage Magazine* and Cadw leaflets to Welsh castles.

Annual publications
Historic Houses, Castles and Gardens. Index Publications.
Houses and Castles Open to the Public. Automobile Association.

Chronology of historic events

William I (1066-1087)
1066 Battle of Hastings. William crowned, 25th December.
1068 Subjugation of the West.
1069 Subjugation of the North.
1070 Harrowing of the North. Subjugation of the Welsh Marches. Hereward the Wake defeated.
1072 Malcolm III of Scotland subdued.
1075 Rising of the Earls: Roger of Hereford, Ralph of Norfolk.
1085 Domesday survey.
1086 Great Meeting at Salisbury.
1087 William dies besieging Mantes.
William II (Rufus) (1087-1100). *Third son of the Conqueror*
1088 Rebellion of the barons. Bishop Odo banished. Ranulf Flambard king's favourite.
1093 Malcolm III killed at Alnwick.
1095 Rebellion of Robert Mowbray.
1099 Godfrey of Bouillon takes Jerusalem.
1100 Rufus killed in New Forest.
Henry I (Beauclerc) (1100-1135). *Youngest son of the Conqueror*
1101 Invasion of Robert of Normandy
1102 Rebellion of Robert Belleme crushed.
1106 Robert of Normandy captured at battle of Tenchebrai.
1120 Prince William drowned in White Ship.
1126 Roger, Bishop of Salisbury, supports Matilda.
1134 Death of Robert of Normandy (eldest son of the Conqueror).
1135 Death of Henry, caused by lampreys.
Stephen (1135-1154). *Nephew of Henry I*
1135 Stephen seizes the throne. CIVIL WAR.
1138 Defeat of David I at the Battle of the Standard.
1139 Invasion of Matilda supported by Robert, Earl of Gloucester.
Matilda (1141). *Daughter of Henry I*
1141 Stephen a prisoner after the Battle of Lincoln. Robert of Gloucester exchanged for Stephen.
Stephen
1147 Death of Robert of Gloucester. Matilda to Normandy.
1153 END OF CIVIL WAR. Treaty of Wallingford.
1154 Death of Stephen.
Henry II (Plantagenet) (1154-1189). *Son of Matilda*
1162 Thomas à Becket Archbishop of Canterbury.
1164 Constitutions of Clarendon.
1170 Murder of Becket at Canterbury.
1171 Richard Strongbow, Earl of Pembroke, to Ireland.
1174 Henry's scourging at Becket's tomb. Ranulf de Glanville captures William the Lion, the king of Scotland, at Alnwick.
1183 Rebellion of Henry's troublesome sons Richard and John.
1189 Death of Henry.
Richard I (Lionheart) (1189-1199). *Son of Henry II*
1190 Richard sails to Crusade. Persecution of the Jews (York).
1199 Death of Richard while besieging Chalus.
John (Lackland) (1199-1216). *Son of Henry II*

1200 William Marshall, Earl of Pembroke, takes office.
1203 Murder of Prince Arthur, John's heir and nephew.
1204 Normandy lost.
1206 Stephen Langton elected Archbishop of Canterbury.
1208 England laid under the Pope's Interdict.
1209 John excommunicated.
1214 Battle of Bouvines.
1215 Magna Carta signed at Runnymede. JOHN'S CIVIL WAR.
1216 Invasion of Louis, Dauphin of France. Hubert de Burgh holds Dover. Death of John.

Henry III (1216-1272). *Son of John*
1216 William Marshall, Earl of Pembroke, regent. Henry aged nine.
1217 Louis defeated at Lincoln.
1219 Death of Earl of Pembroke. Hubert de Burgh in power.
1224 Revolt of Falk de Brent.
1227 Henry, nineteen, declares himself of age. Peter des Roches, Bishop of Winchester, Henry's guardian (1216-27).
1232 Fall of Hubert de Burgh.
1234 Fall of Peter des Roches.
1236 Henry marries Eleanor of Provence; Simon de Montfort one of many unpopular invaders at court.
1240 Death of Llywelyn ap Iowerth, 'The Great', Prince of North Wales (1173-1240).
1257 Richard, Earl of Cornwall, son of John, crowned 'King of the Romans'.
1258 Provisions of Oxford, drawn up by earls of Gloucester, Hereford, Leicester, and William Valence, Earl of Pembroke.
1263 CIVIL WAR. Rebellion of de Montfort.
1264 Battle of Lewes.
1265 De Montfort's Parliament. De Montfort defeated at Evesham.
1272 Death of Henry.

Edward I (Longshanks) (1272-1307). *Son of Henry III*
1272 Llywelyn ap Gruffydd, grandson of Llywelyn the Great, refused homage to Edward.
1277 Edward's first Welsh campaign. Llywelyn surrenders.
1282 Second Welsh campaign: Llywelyn killed.
1283 Dafydd, Llywelyn's brother executed. Edward's great Welsh castles begun. Statute of Rhuddlan.
1284 Birth of Edward, Prince of Wales, at Caernarfon to Eleanor of Castile.
1290 Death of the Maid of Norway, betrothed to Edward, Prince of Wales.
1291 John Balliol elected king of Scotland.
1295 'The Model Parliament'.
1296 Death of William Valence, Earl of Pembroke. Balliol dethroned after the Battle of Dunbar.
1297 Wallace defeats the Earl of Warenne at Stirling Bridge.
1298 Edward defeats Wallace at Falkirk.
1301 Roger Bigod (1245-1306), Earl of Norfolk, reigns as Marshal.
1305 Wallace captured, and executed at Tyburn.
1306 Rising of Robert Bruce.
1307 Death of Edward, while marching on Scotland.

Edward II (1307-1327). *Son of Edward I*

1307   Piers Gaveston, favourite, Earl of Cornwall.
1308   Gaveston exiled.
1310   Power to the 'Lords Ordainers', under Thomas, Earl of Lancaster.
1311   Gaveston surrenders at Scarborough to Earl of Lancaster.
1312   Gaveston executed by Guy de Beauchamp, Earl of Warwick, and the Earl of Lancaster. Hugh de Despencer, favourite.
1314   Battle of Bannockburn.
1321   Despencer exiled.
1322   Lancaster captured at Boroughbridge, and executed. Edward triumphant. Despencer restored.
1326   Invasion of Isabel and Mortimer; Despencer captured and executed. Edward forced to abdicate.
1327   Edward murdered at Berkeley Castle. Accession of Edward III aged fourteen years.

Edward III (1327-1377). *Son of Edward II*
1327   Roger Mortimer, 1st Earl of March, and Isabel rule together.
1328   Edward marries Philippa of Hainault.
1330   Edward asserts himself. Mortimer seized at Nottingham and executed at Tyburn. Birth of Edward, the Black Prince.
1333   Edward defeats the Scots at Halidon Hill.
1337   HUNDRED YEARS WAR.
1340   Birth of John of Gaunt (Ghent). Sea-battle of Sluys.
1346   Battle of Crecy. Defeat of the Scots at Neville's Cross.
1347   Fall of Calais.
1348   Black Death.
1356   Battle of Poitiers.
1376   Death of Black Prince.
1377   Death of Edward III.

Richard II (1377-1399). *Son of Black Prince, grandson of Edward III*
1381   The Peasants' Revolt. Wat Tyler leads the march on London.
1383   Michael de la Pole, Lord Chancellor (1383-6).
1386   Chief ministers: Thomas, Duke of Gloucester; Michael de la Pole, Earl of Suffolk; Robert de Vere, Earl of Oxford.
1387   Gloucester and party defeat the king's forces at Radcot Bridge; de Vere and de la Pole flee.
1389   Richard seizes power for the Crown.
1394   Death of Anne of Bohemia, Richard's queen and creator of fashions.
1396   Richard marries Isabella, eight-year-old daughter of the king of France.
1397   Quarrel of Henry of Hereford and Thomas Mowbray, Duke of Norfolk.
1399   Death of John of Gaunt, Earl of Richmond, Duke of Lancaster by marriage (1362), third son of Edward III and uncle to Richard II. Richard confiscates the Lancaster estates. Henry of Hereford, son of John of Gaunt, lands at Ravenspur.

Henry IV (1400-1413). *Son of John of Gaunt; grandson of Edward III. Earl of Hereford by marriage to Mary Bohun*
1400   Richard's supporters defeated at battle of Cirencester. Richard murdered at Pomfret (Pontefract). Uprising of Owain Glyndwr.
1402   Henry Percy defeats Scots at Homildon Hill.
1403   Revolt of the Percys. King Henry prevents union of Northumber-

land and Glyndwr at Battle of Shrewsbury. 'Hotspur' slain in the battle.

1404 Death of William of Wykeham, Bishop of Winchester (1367-1404); Chancellor, 1368-71, 1389-91.

1405 Henry Percy rebels again. Warkworth, Berwick and Alnwick assaulted by King Henry.

1408 Henry Percy, Earl of Northumberland, (1342-1408) killed at Bramham Moor.

Henry V (1413-1422). *Son of Henry IV*

1414 John of Lancaster, Duke of Bedford, third son of Henry IV, governor in Henry's absence. Lollards meeting in St Giles's Fields. Sir John Oldcastle, Lord Cobham, denounced by Thomas Arundel, Archbishop of Canterbury.

1415 Battle of Agincourt.

1416 Henry Percy, son of 'Hotspur', restored to his estates.

1419 Richard Whittington, Lord Mayor of London for the third time.

1422 Death of Henry.

Henry VI (1422-1461). *Son of Henry V and Catherine of France*

1422 Henry aged nine months. Henry V's brothers the Duke of Bedford, and Humphrey, Duke of Gloucester, responsible for government of England and France. Henry Beaufort, Bishop of Winchester, the young king's tutor.

1428 Fifth Earl of Warwick, Richard de Beauchamp, the king's tutor.

1431 Joan of Arc burnt at the stake.

1435 Death of Duke of Bedford. Richard, Duke of York, regent in Normandy.

1441 Eleanor Cobham, wife of Duke of Gloucester, prosecuted for witchcraft, imprisoned at Chester, then Kenilworth.

1445 Marriage of Henry and Margaret of Anjou, by arrangement of William de la Pole, Earl of Suffolk.

1447 Humphrey, Duke of Gloucester, arrested.

1447 Death of Henry Beaufort.

1448 William de la Pole supreme.

1450 Jack Cade's rebellion in Kent. Death of William de la Pole. Duke of Somerset chief adviser.

1452 York demands removal of Somerset.

1453 END OF HUNDRED YEARS WAR. Richard, Duke of York, Earls of Salisbury and Warwick, and the Duke of Norfolk oppose the king, the Duke of Somerset, the Earl of Northumberland, and Lord Clifford.

1454 York appointed Protector during Henry's illness. Somerset sent to the Tower. Henry regains his sanity and dismisses York and releases Somerset.

1455 WARS OF THE ROSES. Battle of St Albans: York kills Somerset.

1459 Battle of Bloreheath: Queen Margaret's army routed by Yorkists. Battle of Ludlow: Yorkists defeated, York flees.

1460 Battle of Northampton: Warwick defeats queen's army. York claims the throne for his heirs. Battle of Wakefield: Richard of York killed. Earl of Salisbury beheaded. Second battle of St Albans: Queen Margaret defeats Warwick and southern Yorkists.

1461 Battle of Mortimer's Cross: Edward, Earl of March, eldest son of Duke of York, defeated Lancastrians. Edward takes London with support of Warwick and is proclaimed king.

Edward IV (1461-1483). *Eldest son of Richard, Duke of York*

1461 Battle of Towton. Warwick defeats the queen's army. Deaths of Earl of Northumberland and Lord Clifford.

1464 Battles of Hedgeley Moor and Hexham. Warwick crushes opposition to Edward. Henry VI captured and imprisoned. Richard Neville, Earl of Warwick, 'the Kingmaker', supreme. Edward marries Elizabeth Woodville. Quarrels between Woodvilles and Nevilles result.

1468 Warwick plots with George, Duke of Clarence, brother of King Edward.

1470 Revolt of the Earl of Warwick. Alliance of Warwick and Queen Margaret. Warwick and Clarence land at Dartmouth. Warwick releases Henry VI.

1471 Earl of Warwick killed at Battle of Barnet. Queen Margaret defeated at Battle of Tewkesbury. Prince Edward murdered. King Henry VI dies.

1478 George, Duke of Clarence, dies in the Tower.

1483 Death of Edward IV.

Edward V (1483). *Son of Edward IV and Elizabeth Woodville*

1483 Edward aged thirteen years. Edward taken into the care of his uncle Richard, Duke of Gloucester, in the Tower. Joined there by his brother, Prince Richard. Richard of Gloucester declared Protector.

Richard III (1483-1485). *Son of Richard, Duke of York. Married Anne, daughter of Warwick, the Kingmaker*

1483 Richard assumes the Crown. Duke of Buckingham prepares Richard's overthrow. Duke of Buckingham captured and executed at Salisbury.

1485 Henry Tudor lands at Milford Haven. Battle of Bosworth. Richard killed. END OF WARS OF THE ROSES.

Henry VII (1485-1509). *Son of Edmund Tudor and Margaret Beaufort*

1486 Henry marries Elizabeth of York.

1487 Battle of Stoke.

1499 Execution of Perkin Warbeck.

1509 Death of Henry VII.

Henry VIII (1509-1547). *Second son of Henry VII*

1513 Battle of Flodden.

1536 Pilgrimage of Grace.

1539 Dissolution of larger monasteries.

1547 Death of Henry VIII.

Edward VI (1547-1553). *Only child of Henry VIII and Jane Seymour*

1547 Battle of Pinkie.

1549 Kett's Rebellion.

1553 Death of Edward.

Mary I (1553-1558). *Daughter of Henry VIII and Catharine of Aragon*

1553 Lady Jane Grey proclaimed queen.

1554 Wyatt's Rebellion.

1558 Loss of Calais. Death of Mary.

THE CIVIL WAR

Charles I (1625-1649). *Son of James I*

1637 Trial of John Hampden.

1642 Arrest of the Five Members. Royal standard raised in Nottingham. Battle of Edgehill.
1643 Battle of Chalgrove Field. Battle of Lansdown. Battle of Roundway Down. First Battle of Newbury.
1644 Battle of Marston Moor. Parliament victorious. Siege of Gloucester. Second Battle of Newbury.
1645 Battle of Naseby. Parliament victorious.
1646 Charles surrenders to Scots.
1648 Renewal of war. Battle of Preston. Parliament victorious.
1649 Execution of Charles I.

Index

INDEX